To Karen & David —

Continue to be
that 'Positive Spirit
alive!

Dan Druen

Sometimes We Flew

A Fighter Pilot's Tall Tales

By

Dan Druen

Sometimes They Flew

ISBN Number
0-9638455-3-5

Library of Congress Catalog Card Number
95-61858

Warwick House

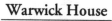

Publishing

720 Court Street
Lynchburg, Virginia

I dedicate this book to my family for their encouragement, assistance patience and support. Without them, it wouldn't have been possible.

I want to thank Nicole Backus for her support and her design of the book's cover and flyer. Also, to Mike Filliman and Andy Olman for their loan of some of the pictures I didn't take, way back then.

These stories are as I remember them with just a little twist here and there to help cover some moments of CRS on my part. It is not my intention to down play anyone's part or diminish anyone's contribution to those wonderful fighter years. If your version of any of these stories differ, I will understand as I hope you will. As a very wise and good friend once told me, "If there's any conflict, let's just not be in the same crowd telling the same war story!"

Dan Druen

Prologue

During the many years of aerial combat, only a limited number of fighter pilots achieved "ace" status. However, hundreds of outstanding fighter pilots accomplished noteworthy feats in their careers. They may not have shot down the five enemy aircraft required to attain the esteemed status of fighter ace, but they acquitted themselves so admirably, bravely, or in such unique fashion that their stories deserve special niches in the history of tactical aerial aviation. This book is about a few of those stalwart fellows and some of their least known exploits. In fact, some of these exploits would, in some cases, be better left untold. But that would be totally unfair to those so deserving. Why shouldn't the public become aware of a few of the lighter moments that went to make up long, long periods of what some called boredom?

Fighter flying is an excitement that only those who experience it can really appreciate. It is a total absorption of mind and body that overcomes you when actually in the cockpit of a fighter plane. But there were also those lighter moments which occurred either in the air or on the ground that made up the total fighter pilot's life, and these are what this book is all about. It is said that when you work hard, you also play hard. Well this may or may not be true, but never let it be said that fighter pilots don't have a sense of humor or don't know when to smile at life, for they do!

These stories offer a brief look at aviation history but they are relevant today because, fighter pilots haven't really changed very much. Even though the technology has taken great leaps and bounds, pilots still have a sense of daring and a devil-may-care attitude even though their leaders may wish a more responsible and mature approach would have evolved with the passing of time. If that had occurred, I am afraid that it would have been the termination of what we know as a real "Fighter Pilot."

I believe a fighter pilot is an individual that is capable of achieving the impossible with the least effort. He is able to do all those things that would take a crew of six to do in a B-52 or a crew of whatever in any other aircraft that has more than one seat. He is the epitome of the human machine when it comes to handling the equivalent of hundreds of horses bundled into one small aircraft called a fighter plane. He is the bombardier, navigator, and driver all wrapped into one; he can do it all and still have time to enjoy what life is all about.

Not everyone has the opportunity to become a fighter pilot nor does everyone who has the opportunity make the grade. That does not mean that the fighter pilot spirit of accomplishment doesn't exist in the hearts of many. It does and that is why this country has been extremely successful in aviation and other walks of life that require an individual effort to succeed. That spirit can take the least likely individual and give him or her the drive to excel and have a good time in the process. It is why we can smile at despair and still land on our feet, even though at times it looks as if things will never straighten out. So maybe some of these tales will relate to you even though you never soared among the clouds, strapped to several thousand pounds of thrust, doing what any free spirit would do if given the chance to really be hanging on to a tiger by the tail.

May that spirit continue in the ages to come and may those of you who don't actually get the chance to do the real thing continue to have the desire and drive to be the navigator, bombardier, and driver of your life. Without that internal spark, we could become just a bunch of sheep waiting for the herd to lead us to the cliff's edge, and then it would take only a little push to put us all over the brink. It's not wrong to have leaders, but lets be sure that we don't stop thinking for ourselves. We must be in control of our destiny or we may as well be on a bomber crew!

Contents

Part One Korea

Part Two Nellis

Part Three Philippines

Part One

KOREA

The Korean Conflict was waged for several years and was a bitterly contested war that saw many good warriors bite the dust. The ground war moved up and down the peninsula of Korea, finally stabilizing at the 38th Parallel, while the air war had the freedom to range over the entire territory south of the Yalu River. The U. S. Air Forces involved, mainly in the tactical portion, were the first US jets to see combat and included the F-80 Shooting Star, the F-84 Thunderjet, and the F-86 Sabrejet. There were other types—some that had accomplished yeoman work during World War II—such as the P-51, B-26, and B-29 that also had major roles. Other jets, like the F-94 all weather fighter, had minor roles but did see some action during that time frame. However, the occurrences that follow are mainly about the tactical side of the conflict and the people who were involved. These stories are about a few of the pilots and their friends who passed through that conflict and left their mark both on the ground and in the air. There is no intent to minimize the outstanding contributions made by any unit, aircraft, or individual. It's just a snapshot of time during 1952 which captures only a few of those lighter moments that encompassed several years of conflict.

"Combat is Hell"

Combat can have a very great impact on a young person's life. The first experience is probably more intense because most pilots have anticipated and trained a long time before seeing those first shots fired in anger. I had barely missed WWII, but now I was here for the real thing in Korea. I had just completed Aviation Cadet Training, and had been commissioned a Second Lieutenant. My final aircraft in flight training had been the P-51. However, when our class graduated, the Air Force decided to check us out in jets, prior to sending us to combat. After upgrading, we completed combat crew training at Nellis AFB, in Las Vegas, and were off to war.

The trip to Japan was made on a DC-6 transport operated by Flying Tiger Airlines. The plane was loaded with pilots and troops headed for the bases in Korea. Time went by slowly, but we were able to get a card game going in the back of the aircraft near the aft loading door. This caused a lot of foot traffic back and forth in the aisle, which continually altered the aircraft's trim. Finally, the aircraft's captain sent one of the male stewards back to insist we limit our movements, or he would have the steward shut down our game. In one voice, we told him to 'get lost.' If there were any more complaints about our actions, we threatened to toss the entire crew out the back door! What were they going to do to us? Make us Second Lieutenants and send us to Korea?

My assignment, after arriving in Japan, was to the famous 4th Fighter Wing, at Kimpo airfield just on the outskirts of Seoul, the capital of South Korea. I was posted to "A" Flight in the 335th Fighter Squadron. The squadron had some top-notch combat veterans flying F-86 Sabrejets. Everyone was expected to do their share. The lives of my buddies could depend on how I performed when the chips were down. It was time to fish or cut bait, and I was wondering just how I would stand up to the pressures of combat.

I checked in at squadron operations, and picked up my personal gear. I caught a weapons carrier to the top of the hill, and got off in the squadron area where the flight billets were located. I made my way down a narrow walkway to the small quarters assigned to "A" Flight. It wasn't what you would call the "Top of the Mark." It was more of a cross between a shack from Tobacco Road, and what was left after the San Francisco earthquake. I entered a fairly drab concrete room with canvas cots outlining the entire perimeter. A large table dominated the center of the room, leaving just enough space at the end for a pot-bellied stove, the room's lone heat source during winter. The place was deserted, the flight was on a mission up to the famed Yalu River. I found an empty bunk in the corner and arranged my sleeping bag to be as comfortable as possible.

No sooner had I finished putting my things away, when the door slammed open and in walked the Flight Commander and the rest of "A" Flight. All I received as a greeting was a couple of nods, and a quick hello, glad to have you aboard. Each member went directly to his bunk and dropped down in what appeared to be complete exhaustion. Immediately they each reached down and pulled out bottles of either Seagrams 7, Canadian Club, or some similar brand of dark bottled whiskey and proceeded to chug-a-lug the contents. This was accomplished without grimace or pause, just a smack of the lips and "Boy was that good." I was in awe. I knew I was capable of flying high and fast, I felt I could hold up my end of any air battle, but I wasn't sure I could drink like that or if, "Horrors of Horrors," combat put that much pressure on your system. Well, needless to say, my first night was without much sleep as I spent most of it tossing and turning and wondering if I could meet the call when my turn came to fly and fight.

The next morning the flight was off to an early briefing. I was told to get settled in, and to be ready for an orientation flight later in the day. There were a total of five such flights that had to be completed before one was considered combat capable. The first three were mostly formation maneuvers of all types; close, spread, and fighting wing. The last two were actual combat sorties north of the 38th Parallel, but not all the way up to the Yalu. But for now, I expected to be alone for the entire morning, just as the day before. However, shortly after the flight departed, the 'Room Boy' arrived to police up the bunks and get rid of last night's trash and debris. He also, to my surprise, reached below each bunk and pulled out the whiskey bottles and started to take them away. Naturally I yelled, "Where do you think you are going with those?" He replied quickly, in his best Korean/American, "To flill them with Vater, just rike I arvays do."

What a relief! I could relax, I wasn't on a fast track to AA. I only had to look forward to a 100 mission tour and the normal amount of alcohol intake. It took a lot of the pressure off right from the beginning, although there was some world class whiskey drinking involved from time to time, but that's a later story!

2

"Nifty's Mig"

There were some fighter pilots who flew their first tour in Korea in the North American P-51 Mustang, sometimes called the Spam Can, but by then it was designated the F-51. It had been a stalwart in WW-II and was still a major weapons system. In Korea, it was used mainly in the air-to-ground role and saw little action as a possible Mig killer. However, one or two of the luckier Mustang pilots did come into contact with Migs on a few occasions. One such case involved a unique fighter pilot by the name of Nifty McCrystal. Nifty was one of a kind. He was the wiry type. He knew how to handle himself in the air, and on the ground. His imagination was fantastic and was rivaled only by his sense of humor.

I really only got to know him after I had returned from Korea and we were both instructor pilots in the same combat crew training squadron. Have you ever seen a cross between a college professor and a mad scientist? Probably not, but that is what Nifty seemed to portray. He was meticulous about almost everything, but his automobile topped the list. He would get with a friend and take the car on the bumpiest road in the area. They would chase down every squeak and sound to insure a tight and noiseless machine. It was an old Cord, with the shiny aluminum exhaust funnels coming out on each side of the engine cover. He kept that car in a spit and polish condition. His attitude for the day could almost be gauged by whether the dust had been wiped off the gleaming surface that morning or not.

At the same time, his attire might range from mod to totally informal. Most of the time he was in an old flying suit, but occasionally he would suit up in his finest for a squadron function. That's when he would walk in with "Mother" on his arm. "Mother" was his wife! She was a petite Japanese lady who Nifty had met on an earlier tour in Japan. He claimed that he liked to sit on cushions and that's why he had married "Mother." A frequent passing comment from him was: "How much allowance does your wife give you?" Regardless of the answer, he would always retort: "Gee, that's more than I get, I've got to tell 'Mother' that I need a raise."

He was the type who legend just seemed to grow around. Many of the tales that he told or that were told about him, could be a bit far fetched. But many of them were also true. It just wasn't always easy to distinguish between the fact and the fiction.

It just so happened that while Nifty was on an Air-to-Ground mission early during the Korean conflict, he had a unique aerial encounter. The mission began as a strafing and rocket attack against some known enemy positions just south of the Chon Chon River, which was about halfway between the Yalu and Seoul. The target, a suspected truck park hidden in the trees, called for strafing first, with the 5" High Velocity Aerial Rockets (HVAR's) to be used last. After three exciting strafing passes, which depleted his ammo, and produced no explosive results, Nifty pulled up high. He wanted to look around and see what attack angle would be best for his rocket deployment. When the name of the game was making match sticks out of wooded areas, Nifty wanted to be sure his passes got the job done. It wasn't every day that allowed a fighter pilot to use his skills to such intricate means.

There had been no earlier calls to warn the Spam-can drivers of any Migs in the area. So, a Mig encounter at this point was the last thing on Nifty's mind. Naturally, the unexpected happened—a Mig appeared from out of nowhere, directly in front of Nifty's F-51. He couldn't believe his eyes; in fact he wasn't sure if it was an illusion or figment of his imagination. Here was the dream of every 51 pilot. A Mig right at his 12 o'clock position, meat on the table, fame for a piston engine driver, and he had just used all of his 50 caliber ammo on a possible (repeat, possible) enemy position. Obviously the Mig pilot wasn't aware of his predicament, which gave Nifty a little time to try to solve his dilemma. His only alternative was to use the 5" HVAR's. He took dead aim—and fired the full salvo of eight directly at the Mig's tailpipe. Now, 5" HVAR's were not what you might call swift and true projectiles. They had what could be termed as very spectacular and erratic flight paths, and this salvo was no exception. The missiles virtually covered the Mig, they went by on both sides, above and below, they were literally all over the place. They came very, very close, but alas, they didn't make contact. The Mig seemed to shudder from the closeness of the rockets, their blazing motors looking like giant fireflies disappearing towards the horizon. The pilot's attention had been peaked, he wasn't sure just what had passed him by, but he didn't intend to wait for a second chorus. In a matter of milliseconds he was into full throttle, zooming towards the stratosphere, like a homesick rocket.

Well, Nifty didn't get his Mig. It had been a once in a lifetime opportunity, but he wasn't downcast. His outlook went this way: Nifty would hold his hands up to his eyes with his fingers and thumb making very large circles around startled eyes. He would say, "When I go on my next trip to Hong Kong and run into an Oriental pilot with the biggest round eyes you've ever seen, then I will know I have found my Mig pilot! I may even buy him a drink; he probably still needs one to calm his nerves." Nifty always looked on the positive side. If you can't kill the guy or scare him to death, the least you can do is change his slanted, to a rounded, outlook on life!

3

"Silence Can Be Golden"

We were on a Combat Air Patrol (CAP) along the south side of the Yalu River looking for Migs, which on this day were not in great evidence. The sky was a sparkling blue, you could see for miles, particularly to the North into Manchuria. The three main Mig bases were in an area immediately north of the river. They were some of the best looking, well built, concrete runways you've ever seen. All of the airspace north of the river was supposedly a "Sanctuary" for the Bad Guys, although there had been a few cases of what you could call poaching in that area. We were supposedly in a war or police action or something that would make you think it was legal to smite those bad guys when and where you could find them, although that viewpoint was not always agreed to by many of the high command. The enemy always seemed to have open season on us in any location, but then we do seem to play with odd rules from time to time.

There had been some slight activity in the area of the Mig fields; the probability of the Migs getting airborne was high. There were fighter bombers working targets not to far south of the river and this usually brought some activity. Had B-29's been up, every Mig in Manchuria would be trying to get into the air. They really loved trying to attack those BUF's (Big Ugly Fellows). The precise details of aircraft movement was difficult to see from thirty thousand feet, so the practice of carrying binoculars in the cockpit had come into vogue. On this particular day one enterprising young jock, equipped with his trusty spy-glasses, decided to become an on-the-spot commentator. He began to give a running observation on the activity at Antung, which was the middle base of the three, or center field, as it was called in our difficult to decipher air code!

In the clear with all the world to hear, the following running commentary began, "The pilots are walking to their aircraft at Antung".... hotdog, some action after all today. "They are starting engines at Center Field".... (there went our intricate code). Now with this second announcement you could almost feel the tension rise and at the same time see the Sabre Pilots jockeying to be in the area of possible action. "They are taxiing at Center Field".... the killers were gathering to insure the best attack positions if and when the Migs decided to come

8

across the river and fight. "They are approaching the number one position for take-off".... now it was imperative that you watched out for other friendly aircraft in what was becoming a very crowded sky just south of the Yalu River. "They are taking the runway".... the tension was building. "They are starting their take-off roll".... you could have heard a pin drop. "They just ..... ABORTED!" It was like a beautiful vision that had just vanished before your eyes, someone had pulled the rug out from under you, the balloon had just burst, there wasn't going to be any joy in Kimpoville tonight.

Unseen by the many, but just as the Migs were burning their brakes to stop on the runway at Antung, two shiny Sabres came flashing down that scene, going like the wind, ready to pounce on what was to have been two airborne enemy aircraft. A calm, but totally disgusted, steely voice was heard to say, "If you had kept your damn mouth shut, they would have taken off!" Thus went another chance of tilting the score just a little bit more in our favor; do you reckon someone was listening? At least that sacred airspace, just north of the river, was spared the pollution from the smoke of two burning Migs; such a shame!

4

"Some Just Won't Fly"

The day was like any other in Korea, kind of overcast and cool, not raining but with a hint of moisture in the air. The afternoon mission was taxiing out, the aircraft were taking off to the north, which was usual. Mobile Control (a small unit close to the runway for on-scene supervision) had been positioned at the north end in preparation for the landings that would be made to the south when the aircraft returned. It was also able to observe the take-offs to make sure everyone got safely airborne.

Everything was going swimmingly with two ship elements blasting off in formation at regular intervals, their black smoke trailing behind as they winged their way north, towards the Yalu. One of the flight elements contained Ape and Jack, buddies from way back. Ape was a five foot ten bundle of dynamite, with steel blue eyes. Jack, a sandy haired dynamo, bordering on perpetual motion. They were a real pair who could set back any group of fun loving troops with their brand of humor. But today they were flying together as numbers 3&4, which made them the last element in the last flight of four. They had reached the runway and were ready for take-off.

When one thinks of an All American Boy, Ape would not be the first person to come to mind. He looked the part but when it came to performance, he exceeded all expectation. He could do a good imitation of the last angry man, but deep down he liked people more than it appeared he did. He could even put up with a few people that didn't fly airplanes, but only for short periods of time. He could be the perfect stand-in for a middle linebacker—the no-necked, beady-eyed, broad shouldered type that would rather knock you on your can than shake your hand.

From the word go, it was either like Ape or not like Ape. He really didn't care how others felt, he picked his friends from the few that he wanted to associate with. The rest could drop off the end of the earth as far as he was concerned. There was no neutral ground for the faint hearted. Luckily, most people liked him, for it would have been very tacky to have a bunch of individuals hanging around with bent noses. He had a slight tendency to take exception to any loud mouth that crossed his path—usually in the form of an altercation which sent the loud mouth scampering for medical attention.

But deep down, he was what has been described as the "salt of the earth." That true friend who could be counted on regardless of the time or situation. He would be there for you when others might shy back. If you were close to right, he would take your side when the popular course dictated caution. And if a drinking buddy was needed, he could and would stay at the bar until the cows came home. But his greatest asset was, he could fly airplanes as well as anybody in this man's air force.

Jack had done his time in the Training Command. He was a WW II veteran who had seen just a bit of combat during the last stages of the European War. He was typical of the many fighter types who had been discharged right after VJ-Day. They had wanted to stay in, but the reduction in force had sent them back to civilian life that prior to flying school had been street corners and drugstore soda fountains. Now, it was either go to school or get a job. Sadly, there just weren't a lot of positions out there that required the talents of an ex-P-51 driver.

He and some buddies decided to beat the system instead of selecting those normal courses that would lead to fame and fortune. They aspired to win the Bendix Trophy race and leap into aviation glory in one fell swoop. They pooled their monies and bought a surplus P-51. The seller even included a spare engine. Fame was only several pylons away. As fate would have it, both engines blew and Jack was lucky to make not one, but two, deadstick landings without rearranging his anatomy.

The Korean conflict was to some, an awful continuation of the bloody business of war. But to Jack, it was the chance that he had been waiting for, a chance to really get back into the sky—the only element that had really been to his liking. He was willing to take any slot as long as it meant being able to fly. It also appeared to afford him that opportunity for the aerial combat that had eluded him over the skies of Germany. Jack was a typical retread who made up a large portion of the US Air Forces in the early 50's—a bit of experience and the willingness to make something happen.

The first time I ever laid eyes on him, he came sauntering into the operations shack at Kimpo airfield. He was a five ten bundle of red haired Irishman, who looked ready to take on the world.

Out at Mobile Control, Lean Leonard, the coolest of characters, had set up shop as the Chief Ground Control

Officer. He was ready to insure proper launches and recoveries. Things were going smoothly, and a little boring—but sleep was out of the question. The roaring engine noise during the take-offs would keep a zombie awake. Watching take-offs wasn't that exciting after you had been there once or twice, but L.L. was on his toes.

The last element was on the take-off roll, charging down the runway just reaching nose wheel lift-off speed. Things were great with one exception—Jack's nose wheel didn't lift off! Now there really wasn't that much runway at Kimpo Airfield and what there was, was being eaten up exceedingly fast by Jack's F-86. Ape was in the air and since he was the element leader, he was concentrating on heading north and not on Jack's particular predicament. Which was becoming more critical by the second.

About this time Lean Leonard focused his attention down the runway and saw the last element fast approaching, one F-86 flying and one that looked like a hotrod tricycle with a very negative angle of attack. A negative attitude was possible on earlier F-86A models, if the nose wheel was under inflated or not enough back pressure was applied before reaching lift-off speed. It caused the aircraft to resist the standard principles of flight; and it was evident that this particular tricycle wasn't going to fly today. In fact, Jack really had only two choices: Go straight off the north end of the runway (which had a pretty steep drop into a gravel pit) or try a hard right turn on to a Pierced Steel Planking (PSP) taxiway. Either choice had less than good odds of survival.

It was at this time that the Mobile Control Officer (old L.L.) leaped into action. He stood smartly to attention, calmly lifted his mike, and announced to the Control Tower in a shrill but authoritative voice, "Tower, We Are Having a CRASH." This was supervision at its height, plus it set into motion the required actions to get the fire department moving as well as other interested parties that attend such happenings.

At the same time, old Ape was wondering just what in the world was going on behind him. He was on the radio, trying in vain to get someone to tell him the status of his old and true friend. Jack, of course, had his hands full trying to make the turn onto the corrugated steel planks, lovingly called a taxiway. He was doing just fine at the task until his left main landing gear gave way and collapsed as he contacted the PSP. This ruptured his left external fuel tank, drenching the fuselage in JP-4 (highly flammable jet fuel) and giving him an excellent chance of becoming a sentinel fire for all of the central part of Korea. The stars, however, were in their right zenith for old Jack. The aircraft slid to a stop without torching off and Jack crawled nimbly out, shaken but without a scratch.

Ape was still yelling over the radio, trying to find out if Jack had survived what appeared to be certain death. You see, Jack owed Ape several hundred dollars from their nightly 'Gin Rummy' games. Naturally you can see Ape's concern for his old buddy. If friends won't worry about you, who will?

5

"Halfway to Go"

Fifty missions were behind me, I was halfway through the required 100. I was a neophyte fighter pilot, stationed at Kimpo Air Base in South Korea, and slowly becoming a combat veteran. Some of the first 50 missions had been more memorable than others, but each had given me a growing respect for all the reasons for our being in Korea. The United States Air Force (USAF) mission was fairly well defined, we were delivering bombs and fighting Migs. The ground war was now being waged along the 38th Parallel. There were probes and excursions made all along that line, but for us Mig fighters, little was seen of our Army buddies.

Directly North of Kimpo Air Base, ground forces were positioned along the southern extremes of the Hahn River. The Hahn formed the western portion of the 38th Parallel, and communist troops occupied the northern banks. We didn't know of the activity there, but occasionally we could hear some artillery fire at night. Our launches, North to the Yalu, were always over that part of the territory. We were usually well into our climb to higher altitude when we passed over the river. I guess we just took their protection for granted, and didn't give that part of Korea a lot of thought. For me, that was to change.

We were on alert status at the south end of the Kimpo runway. The alert shack resembled a shanty directly from the old 'Shanty Town,' of song. The day was fair, with the regular pre-scheduled launches proceeding as planned. Normally each of the three squadrons flew three flights of four each morning to provide close cover for a varied number of fighter bomber strikes, plus screen them from any incoming Migs. Only if the situation got extremely hot, would we be scrambled. There hadn't been any un-expected activity up North this morning, so there wasn't any reason to expect the launch of our flight. I was the element leader, or number three man, in a flight of four. The flight was made up of a mixture of F-86F's and F-86E's. I had one of the earlier 'E' models. The flight was ready, whenever a scramble call was received. However, things were very, very quiet. The four of us were just basking in the summer sun. It wasn't everyday that the sun was that nice on the Korean peninsula. It was beginning to look like there wouldn't be any flying before the relief arrived. Then suddenly, the red scramble phone rang.

In a matter of seconds, the ground crews had the starting units cranked-up. I had strapped on my flying gear, and was in the cockpit with my finger depressing the starter button. The Sabre roared into life. The adrenaline in my veins started to subside only, as the flight received clearance for take-off. That first rush to start and take-off always got the old heart pumping at top speed. The lead element didn't spare any horses as their black exhaust curved north off the runway. Number four and I were right behind them. To make sure join-up could be completed in the least possible time, I held our element on the deck to build up closing airspeed. Our element flashed over the Hahn River at minimum altitude, like two silver arrows with fire for tail feathers.

Parachute and safety straps were normally attached prior to launch, or at least, mine had been. There were times when those details were left to be completed after becoming airborne, just to shave time off the scramble sequence. Not really a smart practice, but it did occur at various times. However, this time, I was securely fastened to all the proper attachments. Somebody must have been watching out for me!

Our element was only seconds north of the Hahn, maybe thirty at the most. I had just started to ease into a climb to join with the leader and his wingman. When suddenly, I was slammed forward in my shoulder harness. What the **H—-**! My God, I had just flamed out! Of all the places to have this happen. Over the land of the 'Bad Guys,' and only feet above the ground. I was going like a bat, but I was headed deeper into 'No No' territory. Instinctively, I yanked back on the stick, and pulled the aircraft into a maximum performance chandelle. This maneuver would reverse my direction, and gain me some much needed altitude. I was trading airspeed for altitude. Plus, I wanted to be headed back across that river. I gained several thousand feet in the maneuver, and established the best airspeed for maximum glide distance. I thought I could make the friendly side of the river, but the base was out of the question unless I could get that engine fired-up again. With a full fuel and ammo load, the glide characteristics of this F-86E was kin to a rock. I did jettison the external fuel tanks, but that didn't help much. It was going to be close, even to make the river, and still have enough altitude to eject.

I had attempted my fourth or fifth re-start, without success. I just couldn't get this thing to light up on the

15

emergency or the normal systems. I was running out of ideas, and certainly altitude, at about the same rate.

Doug, my wingman, had turned around and reached my vicinity about a couple of miles north of the river. He offered his input to my predicament. Unfortunately, there weren't any possible solutions that I hadn't attempted. The damn thing just wouldn't re-start. I tried to get any type of fire going in the back end, but the results were the same. Nothing! It was becoming perfectly clear, that if I was to continue in this world, I better think seriously about ejecting.

My trouble was, that for a high chance of survival, ejection should be initiated no lower than a thousand feet above the ground. The ground level in the area was sea level, so my altimeter was an accurate indication of how much room I had. I was passing through one thousand and five hundred feet, and I hadn't crossed the river yet. It was going to be close. Just as the river passed under my wings, the needle on the altimeter sped past the one thousand foot mark. Doug was yelling, "Get out, get out." Thanks a lot!

At what must have been eight hundred and fifty feet in a downward vector, I pulled the ejection handles, and squeezed the seat firing trigger. The canopy came off in a rush of air, and in what seemed to be the same moment, I was up, up and away from the doomed Sabre. That part was more or less foolproof. But, unlike today's automatic sequencing for seat separation and chute opening, I had to accomplish those actions manually. This added time before I could achieve an open chute over my head, and time was space above the ground.

It was amazing, I didn't seem to be in a hurry-up mode. I knew I was tumbling through space, but each task seemed like an action in a slow motion movie. I could focus on a particular close object, but the rest was just a blur. I unbuckled the seat belt, and pushed vigorously away from the seat. I looked for the parachute canopy release, and locked my thumbs through the T-handle. Such a yank, I launched that handle for what must have been a distance mark for T-handles.

I was falling into the unknown, nothing left to be accomplished in the sequence of lifesaving, when Wham, Pop, and Jerk! The chute opened. My focus returned to normal. Uh-oh, I was within a second of landing square in the middle of a rice paddy. It was a welcomed sight, but I didn't want to go face down in that murky, foul mud. Plop, I hit it with both feet slightly apart. I went to a deep knee-bend, and was able to maintain balance. It had been cut a little close, but I was alive and well. But exactly where?

I had crossed the river, but I wasn't sure that it actually indicated the front line boundary. My first thought was, I had better get my stuff together, and head out to some bonafide safe ground. Before I could get to the narrow dike outlining the paddy, several Korean locals materialized from nowhere. Eager hands scooped up my parachute and harness. My dingy was still attached to the parachute harness. The minimum time in the chute hadn't allowed for deployment before making contact with Mother Mud.

After reaching the dike, I reached into my 'G' suit pocket for a full pack of 'Luckies.' I had opened them just prior to the scramble signal. I extracted a dry one from the middle of the damp and soggy pack, offering the remainder to the growing crowd of locals. Like the swish of a magician's wand, they vanished. Just as suddenly, someone produced a Zippo lighter for my cigarette. It was evident that my first greeters were friendly, or longtime smokers.

I was using my best charade techniques to indicate I wanted to get to a road or some sort of motor transportation. All this while, Doug kept buzzing our location at an altitude that made us crouch on each of his passes. I would have called him on my survival radio, but it was someplace behind me with my parachute harness and dingy. I felt sure he had notified the base of my condition, but I wasn't sure I wasn't going to have to walk back to Kimpo. By this time, there must have been fifty to sixty locals behind me. We looked like a parade winding our way along the rice paddy dikes. The phenomenal thing, more joined by the minute. I guess there wasn't a crash everyday of the week, particularly right in their own backyard.

It was only a matter of minutes before I spied an approaching combat patrol of the best looking U.S. Army grunts I had ever seen. It confirmed my geographical location as being with the 'Good Guys.' I had landed right in the middle of the U.S. Army's Third Infantry Division. That blue and white striped diagonal patch sure was a pleasant sight. They formed an escort, as we proceeded towards what I hoped was transportation back to the base. Just as we reached a two tracked, dirt roadway, a Marine helicopter came swooping in. A crewman jumped out and helped me aboard. I yelled my thanks to the Army guys, and as we lifted off, I waved to what must have been at least eighty to a hundred locals. All were waving and at least nineteen smoking. Sorry, I didn't have several

17

cartons I could have distributed, those people were definitely on our side.

The Marine helicopter put me down right in front of the Wing Headquarters of the 4th Fighter Wing. It was a one story cement building that had been the focal point of a few artillery rounds when the ground war had passed back and forth through this area. It was a bit pock-marked, but still serviceable. One, unnamed, Colonel approached with, "What did *you* let happen to the airplane?" Before I could answer, the Wing Commander, Colonel Harrison Thyng said, "Glad to have you back, Dan." Which one of those troops do you think I would follow into hell?

I was whisked off to the hospital. It was really more of an aid station, tucked away in a large Quonset type structure. A little iodine, a large tumbler of 'Old Rot Gut' (which went down like iced tea), and I was back in service. But, 'what happened to the airplane?' was a good question yet to be answered.

I was flying the next day, had to get back up on that horse after being thrown. One week and about four missions later, I was again headed North in another F-86E model. I was scheduled as airborne spare. This meant, I would fill-in, should someone have aircraft trouble prior to reaching the Yalu. I was cruising along at thirty thousand feet, about halfway between Kimpo and the Yalu. When suddenly, my sole source of propulsion, slowly expired. It felt like the air was easing out of a big balloon. Could this really be happening to me again? Immediately, I headed for a safe island off the West coast of North Korea, called Chodo. If I couldn't get this one started, I wanted to be able to eject near some friendlys.

I made the necessary radio calls to notify the proper authorities, then set about trying to get this machine chugging again. After the last experience at low, low level, it seemed like I had all the time in the world. After several attempts, miracle of miracles, I got the engine going on the emergency fuel system. I turned for home, staying close to the coastline. If this thing quit again, I was going for a swim in the South China Sea, and rescue by our Navy. I wasn't about to cut across the North Korean land area.

I stayed at altitude as long as possible. When I could almost see Kimpo, I started my let-down for landing. No sooner had I commenced my descent, than my flame went out. This wasn't my day! It wasn't even my week.

The re-start attempts were to no avail. I was in the glider forces again. I did have altitude, so my chances for a dead-stick landing were good. And, that's just what I did. My touchdown speed, headed south on the Kimpo runway, may have been slightly hot. But, I didn't mind. I was on the ground safely. All I needed was to get this freewheeling tricycle stopped, before running out of pavement. A dead engine certainly helps deceleration, so when the end of the runway arrived, I made the turn off with only a slight screeching of the tires.

As I sat in the cockpit waiting for a tug, my first greeter was my unnamed Colonel friend(?). This time, I beat him to the punch line. "I brought this one back! Now, we all can find out what happened." He only nodded, and refrained from offering another caustic retort. It probably saved him some teeth since I still remembered his last.

The findings of the next few days, determined that the F-86E models had some faulty fuel controls. Immediately, steps were taken to inspect and replace those found defective. Amazingly, our flame-out problem went away, too bad it couldn't have been a few weeks earlier. Thank goodness this episode occurred at my halfway point.

Just think of having to combine Migs, flame-outs, and muddy rice paddies for another fifty. They always said, War is Hell! I guess now I knew what they meant.

6

"On to the Fuji New Grand"

The Rest and Relaxation (R&R) leave from Korea was always looked forward to with great anticipation. It was a badly needed three day break from an otherwise grinding situation (combat) that required some less trying pastime just to keep your values straight. This particular upcoming R&R was no exception, and had been planned to be the Granddaddy of them all. Eight of us, all second lieutenant fighter pilots well into our first combat tour, had contracted for reservations at the Fuji New Grand. It was a plush hotel on the slopes of Mt. Fuji. The money had been paid, all that remained was to arrive on the scene, and have the fun begin. There was one small exception; I had one more mission to fly before we departed. That was no problem, just one short little combat patrol. We would be all set to catch the late night flight out of Kimpo to Tokyo. Everyone was packed and ready.

I was leading the element or flying the number 3 position in a flight of four aircraft. My wingman, number 4, was a troop by the name of Smitty. He hadn't been in the squadron long, but seemed to be more than capable. We were just south of the Yalu River in a wide tactical formation. We were looking for Migs, when from high and behind there appeared an even dozen that were looking for a fight. They wasted no time in starting their attack as they dove toward us. We turned into their approach so we could present them with the highest and hardest possible angle for firing. It worked on the first pass. We had them at an angle that would make them overshoot their intended line of fire. Had they continued, they would have been susceptible to our attack, putting them on the defensive. They, however, were not to be suckered in that easily. They pulled off sharply and went back up to a more ideal position, high and behind us. Ugh!

Their second attack started from a better angle. It really was going to put us in a tight spot, so the flight leader called for a defensive split between the elements. This meant that Smitty and I were to go high and the lead element would go low. This theoretically would split the Migs into manageable groups and free one of our elements to come back and make a counterattack. Unfortunately, the majority of the Migs chose to follow Smitty and me. That really wasn't what we had hoped for. They either had a different tactics manual or we had lost a

20

page from ours. It was evident from the time we made the split that we had our hands full. Migs could out-climb and out-accelerate the F-86. Our only advantage would be to get the Migs to a lower altitude, at which point we could begin to out turn them. In other words, we could become the hunter instead of the hunted, which was our game plan all along.

I said, "Smitty, let's pull it in hard left and take it down," meaning for us to go into a tight spiraling left-hand downward turn. This could possibly draw the Migs to an altitude that would give us (the good guys), a slight advantage.

Back at the base, my seven fair weather friends, with nothing but time on their hands until their departure for R&R, were at the squadron listening to the radio chatter on the squadron's combat frequency. It wasn't the most entertaining pastime in the world. On this day, the ping-pong table was already in use because it was too wet outside to pitch horseshoes. When they heard that Smitty and I had all those Migs "Trapped" at our six o'clock position (an undesirable location for someone who didn't desire to get shot down and had already paid for a reservation at the Fuji New Grand), they really became interested.

Smitty and I were hard at work. We were in that left diving turn and I for one was putting everything I had into making my Sabre do the old-nose-trying-to-catch-the-tail routine. Smitty was lagging a bit, so I was urging him on with, "Smitty, you better pull it tighter or they are going to have your ass!" I thought some down-home logic would do wonders for him. He seemed to do better immediately. We were making progress, but the outcome was still greatly in doubt.

At the squadron, a different scene was unfolding. My friends were rooting for us, but they were also busy looking for a fill-in for my space at the Fuji New Grand. They hadn't completely written me off, but my chances didn't look like I would be making this R&R or any others as far as they could tell. They weren't getting a lot of takers, which meant that their entire scheme would be one person short. Who would they get as a fourth for the second bridge table? Suuuure, we played bridge on R&R's.

By the grace of God and some hard turns, the Migs decided that they were slowly losing the battle of being the shooter and instead were rapidly becoming the shootee. After we got off a few short bursts at their tails, they pulled off and streaked back to their side of the border. It's marvelous what

21

some maximum rate turns and perseverance can do for young fighter pilots!

Boy, was I upset when I returned and found that my slot for the R&R was up for sale. I told them what a fine lot I thought they were and asked just what they would have done since I had already paid my money. They, being the sentimental types they were, said, "Gee, we would have refunded your money. We would have sent it to your Mother with all your other belongings." Now I didn't shed a tear on that pathetic note, but I was glad I made it back. I had no desire to spend an extended R&R as a guest of the North Koreans!

7

"The View From Mt. Fuji"

Well we were off, it had been close but that last combat flight had been worth it even though my buddies(?) were skeptical of me making the scene. We leaped aboard 'Old Shakey' out of the Seoul trash carrier base and arrived at the Tachikawa Air Base on the outskirts of Tokyo with plenty of time to catch our train to the Fuji New Grand. As a matter of fact, we were able to spend several hours in the depot bar before departure time. We spent a lot of time in bars, but only when we weren't flying. Any flight, particularly combat sorties, dictated that you be alert and clear eyed. When survival hinged on being sharp and ready, there was no place for sluggishness brought on by alcohol. That's not to say some pilots might have taken a few flights in less than tip top shape, but it was the exception rather than the rule. We worked hard and played hard, on R&R's we were certainly doing some hard playing.

As luck would have it, we ran into four American girls (round eyes) that were also on their way to the same hotel. There were eight of us, so half would have to look for other forms of recreation. Three were pretty nice looking, but one had a bad case of the 'Uooglies.' We drew straws and David won (?) the honor. It wasn't all that bad, we were just looking for conversation, companionship, and a pretty face. Two out of three was in the ball park.

We were in great shape when the train pulled out of the station, the conductor was so glad to see us that he gave us our own private car. At least that's the way it seemed. All the little Japanese people decided to leave the Club Car, they didn't care to play aisle hockey even though we would've let them have the bar end for their goal. It is really hard to be friendly in a foreign country. Then again, we had whipped their asses just a few years previously. That must be called, 'To the victors go the spoils,' or 'The club car belongs to those who need it the most.'

Arrival at the station below Mt. Fuji was greeted with great joy and relief by all members of the train crew, with the conductor leading the handshakes all around as we departed. The R&R bus was waiting for us and it didn't take any time before we were on our way up the mountain side. On board was a brand new Lieutenant, our escort officer, who was part of the hotel staff. He assured us that our stay would be everything we had anticipated. He had activities planned for the entire visit; Badminton, Croquet, Horseshoes, Hot Baths, and other stimulating exercises to help us enjoy the peaceful and restful atmosphere of the resort. At least he hit one correctly!

The place was gorgeous, the view was spectacular, and the accommodations were plush. If this had been a Japanese resort before the war, they had certainly done it up right. It was a relaxing setting that could take those pent up pangs out of your system. It would have been a little more relaxing if there had been more than four females booked for the same three days. (Actually there were two more already there, which brought the total to six, but the two additional were in the same category as the one David won, so forget it). Soooo......, just lay back and enjoy, remember, no one wanted to be a non-paying guest (POW) in the transient quarters of the North Koreans.

Despite the urging of the Lieutenant, we all made it to the bar instead of the badminton court. We had to get the dust out of our throats after that long ride up the mountain. The next stop was the hot bath area, which was unique in itself. There was a large pool of clear cool water cascading down from rocks that were a part of the mountain. Immediately adjacent was a pool of very hot water. The drill was to soak in the hot water, then dash quickly and dive into the pool of mountain fresh water. Talk about clearing the cobwebs out of the system, that will do it in a New York second. After about six round trips, it felt like the entire universe had been realigned and everything was right with the world. Also available, were individual rooms that contained the normal pool of very warm water. These were for private bathing, although on one occasion, a couple of us were joined by a Japanese family. It sure made for some interesting hand signals, since neither party could speak the others language. So went the exciting first afternoon.

The activity program for the first evening called for dancing in the ballroom after dinner. We could hardly wait, six females and us. It wasn't that bad but it did keep most of us at the bar for the majority of the night. Just when things were getting halfway decent, the Lieutenant came in and said curfew was in five minutes. You have got to be sh—ting me! What was this curfew crap? Unfortunately, he wasn't kidding. The music stopped, the lights were turned to full bright, and we were on our way to bed. As we walked back towards the rooms, we were somewhat boisterous with our comments about this establishment, it's rules, and it's management. The Lieutenant was attempting to quiet us down and was on his second warning. He said, "I've told you once now, you must remember that there are others here from Japanese bases that want to rest from their demanding jobs, so be quiet or I will have to report you." With that, Bobby J. reached over and grabbed the Lieutenant by his shirt front. He pulled him close and said, "OK, you've told us, now get lost or we may toss you off this mountain." That was the last we saw of him for that evening.

With the situation being what it was at the hotel, we wandered down to the little village, and found the Japanese version of a bar. Sake isn't bad if you don't drink too much of it. Unfortunately, we didn't follow that rule, the morning head was tremendous, and even the hot and cold pool applications didn't bring things to an even keel immediately. One thing that had been a unanimous decision just before we finally hit the sack: we were getting out of this place. We weren't about to spend the rest of our R&R adhering to curfews and having some brand new 'Brown Bar' tell us that some noncombatants needed their rest.

We had our bags packed and were in front of the hotel standing by the bus when the Lieutenant came out to see what was going on. We told him our intentions and he countered with, "I sorry, but the bus isn't scheduled for the train station today." We didn't argue with that at all, we just put our luggage in the bus and borrowed it for an hour or two. As we departed, the Lieutenant had a somewhat quizzical look on his face. We couldn't for the life of us understand why, we had told him where he could shove the hotel and pick up the bus. What more information does an individual need?

The ride down the mountain was only one step short of comparing with any of the hairiest combat missions any of us had ever participated in. David had been elected to drive, and he had us off in a cloud of dust before you could say 'Goodbye' in Japanese— 'Saranar.......something.' No one had bothered to tell David that the Japanese drove on the wrong side of the road. We counted two small cars in the ditch, several grazed fenders, and at least fifteen irate bicycle drivers. Luckily we didn't have to wait for the train. It was in the station when we arrived and we lost no time in getting aboard and out of that district.

It was nice to be back in Tokyo, we went directly to our old tried and true family hotel that we had frequented on previous R&R's, the Sun Hotel. It had a nice bar, a good hot bath, adequate rooms, and a beautiful view of the palace moat(?).

R&R's were too precious to leave in the hands of weenie ground pounders. We would never again believe some exaggerated vacation brochure, it might have been written by some 'Brand New Lieutenant' that didn't know 'you know what' from shinola!

8

"The University Club"

While an R&R is a pleasant break in the business of combat, it does get you to a point that makes you so relaxed that you are ready to get back into the routines that made you want the break in the first place. In other words, you can take just so much happiness at any one spell. Then you have to get completely tensed-up again so you can enjoy the next one when the time arrives. Because you need a true cultural shock to get you back in the world of the living, many of our R&R's started and ended at the University Club in Tokyo. It was an officers club located in the center of Tokyo that catered to any and all. It was a particularly popular meeting place for the troops getting a few days off from the grind in dear old Frozen Chosen (Korea). For one thing, you could get a nice Shrimp Cocktail, Filet Steak, and Strawberry Shortcake dinner that was impossible to come by in the mess hall at Kimpo. In fact, you would usually double that order shortly after arrival just to get that good taste in your palate before you went on to greater heights. You would also have a similar meal before returning to Dear Old Kimpo that would hopefully keep your gourmet memory cells alive until your next trip. This particular evening was no exception in that it was our last fling before returning to Korea. It also happened to be just the beginning of a three day adventure for our dear old friends, Ape and Jack. You remember what a caring twosome they were when one owed the other some money?

We were in a back booth, sipping a few bourbon and waters, coasting down from a full, and I mean full, three days of rest (?). We were just trying to mind our own business before going up to eat when in walked Ape and Jack. They were in a festive mood and went directly to the bar without looking around the room to see who they might know or want to know. They could really dominate a room with their fun loving attitude, and this evening was no exception. They ordered doubles with back-up doubles to what appeared to be an already good headstart on an evening that would be one of their more notable ones. Jack went directly to the closest slot machine and began depositing coins. After just a few minutes of pulling on the handle without any cooperation from the machine, Jack was somewhat upset and voiced his dismay to

Ape. "This GD machine doesn't want to payoff," was his first comment that could have been heard across the street. Ape immediately responded. He ambled over to the machine, grabbed it with both hands, pushed it over on its back and banged it up and down two or three times. He said, "Now try it"! On the next coin the machine paid off, luckily for the machine. During all of the going back and forth between the bar and the slot machine, the dynamic duo looked over and spied us in the back booth. Immediately, they were on their way over to be their sociable selves.

The place was so crowded, it took them a couple of seconds to thread their way between the tables. They made it without banging or pushing too many people along the way. As they strode up to the booth, they were a bit boisterous, to the point that the people in the adjoining booths were turning to get a good look at the source of the clatter. There appeared to be a little annoyance by some of the older patrons. For what reason, I would be hard pressed to guess. Who could be upset just because two fun loving fighter pilots were being jovial and disturbing the otherwise staid atmosphere of the University Club? Well, the obvious explanation was some gravel crunchers (non-rated troops) who thought they owned the club were taken back by a little noise, but that didn't phase these two stalwarts. They just carried on as if it was their appointed duty to entertain all these stuffy individuals who lived in the safe confines of Japan. It just so happened that a cute young thing in the adjoining booth turned to look as Jack was greeting everyone in our booth. He was gesturing with his hands, as any fighter pilot is known to do, when he looked directly in her face and said in a volume that was just below the roar of thunder, "I'll F—K ANYTHING THAT MOVES!" Which in those days was tantamount to blaspheme, today it would hardly garner a glance. Immediately the silence in the area was deafening. You could hear the muffled gasps throughout the room as people didn't know whether to laugh or cry. It was then that Ape spread his hands wide as if trying to calm a vast congregation and said, "NOBODY MOVE!" The young thing in the next booth drew back in horror (she moved) but Jack looked straight at her and said, "That's OK, lady. You're safe, I thought you were a pigeon!"

Needless to say, we all departed the bar area for the dining room. We wanted to get that last good meal before they threw us out of the place. It was a fond farewell that we gave Jack and Ape. We never thought they would stay out of trouble, but amazingly they made it back to Kimpo, not any worse for the experience. Somebody must really look after drunks, fools, and fighter pilots, or is that redundant?

9

"So Much For Free Transportation"

Sometimes even the return trip from an R&R can be more than was bargained for. That is just what happened on a particular trip returning from Tokyo to Seoul, a mere two hour flight, that was supposed to be a milk run. We were scheduled to fly back in a C-124, which is a big hulk of an airplane. It had four big engines, and needed every one of them to keep it airborne when fully loaded. It could carry a couple of trucks and supplies plus a whole lot of men crammed into a top deck. It was like being stuffed in a big long pipe with no windows. The cockpit was about three stories off the ground, and if you ever fell out, it definitely wouldn't be very good on the old head bone. It could have been an early beginning for the craze of Bungee Jumping, if safety straps had been attached.

Well on this night, the plane was fully loaded and we were on the top deck, packed in like sardines. It was shoulder to shoulder, and knees to knees. We were a bit tired so we really didn't mind all that much. We could endure almost anything for the short flight back to dear old Korea. As usual, there was a lot of talk about what we thought of 'Trash Carrier' pilots and their aircraft, but we admitted that they were providing us with transport when other means weren't available. The engines had started, and we were taxiing out for take-off. Bill, our eternal voice of facts and figures, leaned over and said, "You know, if just one of these engines were to quit on take-off, we would be history." With that nice thought, all conversation was ended on this dull and rainy evening.

The pilot did a very thorough engine check, which seemed longer than usual, but at last we were finally ready to roll. The engines were at max revolutions, the colossal fuselage was shuddering, the beast was straining at it's leash. Then the brakes were released. It was like the rubber band had broken, the air was seeping out of the balloon, for certain, it wasn't a rocket start. The C-124 didn't make what anyone could call a rapid dash down the runway; in fact, it had one of the slowest, lumbering, and time consuming take-off rolls of any aircraft in the Air Force inventory. After what seemed to be more than enough time to get airborne, we were really rattling and shaking along. From inside that closed upper deck, it finally felt like we were flying. We were on our way, almost feeling the aircraft skimming over the rice paddies, straining to maintain airspeed when SILENCE — all four engines stopped! We all looked at Bill with open mouths, thinking of his fateful comment. Each of us knew we were dead. There was no way out of this impossible trap. We just sat there, waiting for the impact, and the flames to come licking through the fuselage. When suddenly, the engines came alive (in reverse) and the brakes screeched loudly, finally bringing the big lumbering hulk to a stop. It was a long, long few seconds. The pilot had aborted, stopped, decided not to take-off or whatever you want to call that hair-raising maneuver.

We were shaken but alive and couldn't wait to find out just what had occurred. After returning to the ramp, we received an explanation. The engines hadn't been turning up enough torque (?), so the decision was made to abort. Bully for that decision. That pilot was my kind of thinking man.

The requirement to change more than seventy-five percent of the spark plugs in all four engines would delay our departure for more than an hour, so we just laid about since there was no bar in the local vicinity. They did a quick job, and we were ready to go in about the estimated time.

Here we were again, back on board with the same heavy load and on the same upper deck, packed in like the same old sardines. The engine run-up was accomplished with about the same time lapse as before, but there seemed to be a bit of hesitation about trying to get on the runway and making the take-off. Finally, we were on the runway and motoring along at what felt like snail speed. The vibrations were still there, and the duration for a successful take-off had just about been reached when the pilot again cut power. This time it didn't have quite the same effect as before, but it still got our attention and put us only about one step above the 'basket case' category. There was no way we were going to get back on this monster if they ever let us off. We were going to look for other means of transportation. Maybe there was boat traffic going our way or something other than "Old Shakey" for sure. We gathered our gear and headed for the passenger lounge to tell these people what we thought of their operation, their airplane, and their mothers. This was almost as exciting as combat, but it seemed that in combat you had a better chance of survival.

The head "Trash Carrier"(C-124 pilot) met us at the door of the operations building and led us straight to another C-124 before we could get enough rope to hang him. This one was empty of cargo and before we could say no, it had its engines running and we were on our way. That was the only way they could have gotten us in another one of those crowd killers. For sure, we never made another flight in a C-124, and I for one was extremely grateful when I kissed the ground in Korea.

10

"Jackpot Flight"

We were headed North on a hot scramble. There were supposed to be about ten flights of Migs on the south side of the Yalu that were either having maneuvers or just getting in their weekly flying time. There weren't any fighter bombers working anywhere in that vicinity, in fact, there weren't any US types in North Korea. It was late in the afternoon, so I guess they felt it was safe to venture over from their sanctuary. We would be hard pressed to get up there and go a few rounds before the sun went below the horizon, but we were surely going to give it the old 'college try.'

I had filled in as the number four man for a friend that needed to have the afternoon off. It had looked like a non scramble day, and I didn't have anything special pending. All I needed was to be the first guy in the movie line, you had to be sure to beat the 'beatures.' Those were the ones that beat you to chow, beat you to the bar, and beat you to anything that meant standing in line for. Now it looked like I would be beating my friend to a few Migs, would he be upset!

The weather was clear except for a very thin high cirrus deck, with in-flight visibility almost unlimited. Radar was bringing us in over the Yellow Sea fairly low so we could get as close as possible before being picked up by their early warning system. As we came in over land, we climbed to thirty thousand feet and proceeded Northeast towards the big dam approximately fifty miles up the Yalu.

We were at least twenty minutes ahead of the alert flight from the 51st Wing, which was stationed at Suwon, thirty or so miles South of Kimpo. Sometimes it paid to be closer to the bad guys, and this was a good example.

Radar was calling bandits in every quadrant, but we hadn't seen a thing. Maybe they were just figments of the radar guys imagination, or some of those weird ghost blips that show up on the radar screen. At any rate, the sky was void of anything that looked like the enemy! Where were the Migs?

"Let's split up and try to make a wider sweep," came the booming voice of the flight leader. He and his wingman would head back down towards the mouth of the Yalu, while our element would continue Northeast. "Sounds like a good idea to us," responded Jim L., who was leading the element.

We had been classmates in flying school, so we were familiar with each other's flying abilities.

Immediately, we spread our aircraft very wide to give us better visual coverage and still maintain mutual support. We had proceeded another ten miles when suddenly two flights of Migs showed up high overhead in the cons (vapor trails left by the hot engine exhausts referred to as cons or contrails). They were headed South, so we turned to stay below them. We started a slow climb to be at their six o'clock position, while remaining just below the cons. They appeared to be making a long easy turn that would bring them back on the Manchurian side of the Yalu in several more miles. As we tracked their progress hoping they would descend before they got back across, they increased their turn as if to make a beeline for the other side of the river. Either we had been spotted or their radar warned them we were in the vicinity. Their flight level had to be at least forty plus thousand feet, where maneuvering could be critical if the controls were jerked around with a ham fist. Suddenly, tailend charlie over controlled while trying to maintain his proper position and went into a spin. If he didn't recover immediately, he was going to spiral down right in front of us. Without waiting to see what he was going to be able to do, we both pulled our noses up and blasted off a few rounds in his general direction. The tracers (which were spaced every fifth round) showed up brightly in the fading light of day. They must have made an impression on him because he lost no time in ejecting. Immediately his chute opened (the rip cord must have been tied to the seat). He had to be well above thirty-five thousand where the temperature was some low, low degrees below zero. I went zipping by as he hung in his chute. He was in a black leather flying suit which I didn't think was going to be warm enough for his trip down. If he didn't freeze to death before he hit the ground, he was certainly going to be frost bitten on all extremes.

We wheeled around trying to see what the rest of the gaggle was going to do. We could hear our lead element engaged with other Migs further down the river. This was truly a Jackpot group, better than being in Vegas with a free slot machine, and we had them all to ourselves. About forty versus four was a nice round ratio. The 51st's flight was on its way, but they had better hurry if they wanted any part of the action.

Man, we had just begun to fight. "Two going slightly low at two o'clock," I called starting to take a course that would put me on an intercept vector. Jim said, "Roger, have them, let's try for both." We were really motoring with more overtake speed than we needed. Our curve of pursuit put Jim into position to fire first, and he really made the most of it. His Mig sparkled like the Fourth of July and immediately belched fire and smoke. Jim broke hard left, to keep from ending up ahead. I insured our six o'clock position (our tailend) was clear of any over eager Migs, then tried to concentrate on the second Mig. I was almost on top of him with just enough time to get in a short burst. I observed a few rounds hit him hard before I had to pull back on the stick to keep from having a mid-air. The zoom put me high and directly over him. I rolled inverted and observed dual chutes. Jim saw one chute, but must have been out of position to spot the other. No problem, we had others to deal with. There were two more very low and streaking for sanctuary, it would be difficult to get a shot at either of them. Jim was climbing in a steep right turn and I was trying to get back into a mutual support position. We were dashing to get a shot at a flight of four that were out of range when the river made us break off. We wheeled around, coming back to an area just South of the dam. We were in a position to cut off their escape route but amazingly, the sky was clear.

There wasn't a Mig in sight! Where had they all gone? They couldn't have vanished in what seemed to be a blink of the eye—but they had. Combat, for this day, appeared to be over. It had been a few glorious moments, whirling and diving. The caustic smell of gun powder as the six, fifty caliber machine guns spit out their deadly stream of lead. The adrenaline was still pumping but the party was over. It is somewhat like standing very close to the tracks as a fast freight passes by, after it is gone your body can still feel the shaking and rumbling.

Well it hadn't been a Mariana's Turkey Shoot, but it hadn't been all bad either. The flight accounted for four kills, two damages, and one probable. Not too bad for a late evening scramble. Rest assured there were a few victory drinks at the Kimpo O'Club bar that night.

I sure hope that high altitude parachutist made it to the ground. I wonder if the North Koreans had ever heard of 'Hot Buttered Rum'? That guy was going to need about three gallons worth, for sure!

11

"The Good Neighbor Policy"

Kimpo Air Base was the home of the 4th Fighter Wing, but there were other flying units that also resided on that hallowed ground. The 4th occupied the entire east side with its three squadron complement of F-86 Sabre Jets, while the 67th Reconnaissance Wing and the Royal Australian's 77th Squadron were on the west side. The 67th had several types of reconnaissance (recce) aircraft that included RF-51's, RF-80's, and a few RF-86's that were called "Honeybuckets," while the Aussies flew British Meteors. On several occasions we would party with these troops, mostly on nights when the next day's mission schedule was very, very light. However there were exceptions. We would, from time to time, just pop over to the 67th late in the evening for a couple of drinks, and then partake of their midnight breakfast. The breakfast was open to their aircrews and invited guests and served real eggs. Occasionally after a few drinks, we would be invited to have breakfast with them, which was a real treat for us. We only got real eggs in our mess hall on Sunday mornings, when they had the malaria pills laid out that you were expected to take once a week. They must have figured that the two offset each other. I guess they had to bribe you with something, for the odds of getting malaria in the frozen confines of Korea was like winning the Irish Sweepstakes on a single ticket.

Jack, of Ape and Jack fame, had a standing invitation for midnight breakfast from his old buddy Ross. Ross was a big, big Texan who had been with Ape and Jack back in the Training Command days. This particular evening, Jack decided to visit Ross and his 67th buddies. He asked if I wanted to hoist a few and have a breakfast with real eggs. Naturally, I said yes, so off we went. We were just on the early mission, not the early, early one, although Jack was the main briefing officer for the mission.

The evening progressed at the average pace except that Jack was having a slight difference of opinion with one of the recce types. This was creating a bit of a bind because we were just fun loving troops who wanted to have a couple of drinks, a hearty breakfast and get back to our side of the field in time to get some decent crew rest before flying. It seemed that this one individual took exception to us coming over to their area, drinking their booze and eating their fresh eggs. Jack's friend, Ross, was this weirdo's squadron commander, and he had invited us so we were not about to let some sourhead ruin our evening. There were a few bitter words from time to time between Jack and this obnoxious individual I will call Mr. X, but it hadn't really built into anything that would cause us to alter the drinking or the comradeship of the night. This guy was like a disturbed fly; he kept buzzing around and around and just wouldn't go away no matter how much you tried to brush him off. I told Jack, "Ignore him and he will eventually get tired," but by this time Jack was beginning to get his dander up. There were a few comments from both parties that I overheard like, "Without your guns you wouldn't go north of the 38th Parallel," Mr. X was implying that we wouldn't go un-armed like recce troops. Jack's retort was, "How long does it take to get the Honeybucket smell off?," casting the allegation that the recce aircraft was really a "Sh-t" wagon. With such endearing comments on a nice evening with friends, it was evident that something other than drinks and breakfast was in store. It seemed that the only thing that might calm this head-on clash was to eat earlier than planned. We could only hope that this might eliminate a major confrontation over what seemed to be a petty misunderstanding.

It was a scrumptious meal as usual, thoroughly satisfying and not what you could call a low cholesterol menu. Four eggs (over easy), three strips of bacon, three pancakes, two patties of sausage—topped off with all the milk and coffee you could drink. To have such a fine meal on a cold night really warmed the cockles of your heart. It made you want to sit around and just savor the juices forever, but we had to eat and run due to Jack having to lead and brief the early morning mission. We thanked Ross and told him he was welcome at our place anytime. He said he would take a raincheck, knowing we didn't have anything but powdered eggs.

As we came out of the mess hall on the way to our jeep, who was waiting outside in the below freezing weather but dear old Mr. X. This guy really had a chip on his shoulder and there was no way he was going to let Jack leave without some type of altercation. Jack said, "OK, let's get on with it before we both freeze to death," so right there in front of everyone they squared off. Mr. X made a head long run at Jack and Jack hit him with a solid right cross, square on the jaw. Mr. X's momentum carried him into Jack and they both went down on the gravelly surface locked into bear hugs. After rolling around for a few minutes, they decided to let each other up and go at it again. The same routine was repeated several times, Jack hitting X and X grappling Jack to the ground. The gravel on the ground was beginning to take a toll on Jack's face, and the hard rights to X's jaw were making their mark. Well, I had just about all I could take of this so I departed the scene to get the jeep. When I returned, they were still rolling around on the ground, and I said, "If that's all you guys are going to do, let's call it even!" Well you would have thought I said the magic word. Up they jumped, the fight was over, finished, called on the account of cold and waning interest. And I deeply suspected, they both wished someone had said that a lot sooner. To top things off, they offered each other cigarettes and seemed to be the best of friends—crazy people. Jack's face was a bit scratched and X's jaw was a bit swollen (later we learned that it had a slight fracture), but the world was at peace again.

We finally drove out of there and got back to the flight room. In the bright light of our lone stark 100 watt bulb, Jack's face was really a mess, so I started applying iodine. I was being the Rembrandt of "A" Flight, using the cotton applicator like a paint brush. About halfway through the process he began to look like Chief Sitting Bull about ready to go on the war path, and needless to say, I thought it was one of the funniest things I had ever seen. Jack didn't share my amusement, but he did let me complete my masterpiece of iodine on flesh. I finally finished the job and we hit the sack to get at least some small amount of crew rest. We didn't want to over do it.

The next morning at the mission briefing, Jack walked to the briefing podium with his face tucked down into his flying suit collar and immediately turned his back to the flight crews. The briefing sounded like he was talking more to the map than to the fighter jocks. He was really hard to understand, as he tried to talk over his shoulder and not face the throng of troops. The squadron emblem, the head of an Indian Chief adorned in war paint, hung directly over the scheduling board and map that Jack was using. Finally, he couldn't hide it any longer, he had to turn around, and there before God and everyone was good old Jack painted to the hilt. He made the squadron emblem look pale in comparison. The whoops and hollers were something to behold. Jack was a bit upset with my art work, but he flew the mission and did some of his best work; he got two Migs! Maybe it was the war paint?

Later he said that was the last time he would ever take

me to eat breakfast at the 67th, but that was alright. We had both been restricted from ever going over to the 67th area again, anyway! I wonder why?

12

"AT&T Was Never Like This"

"A" Flight didn't have a telephone in its flight room as did "B" Flight. If we wanted to use the phone, we had to go outside, all the way around to the center of the building, sometimes in the wind and rain, just to get to the phone in their room. This wasn't convenient even though part of the adjoining door between our flight rooms had a panel missing. This made it possible to crawl through when all else failed. Most often the "B" flight commander, Champ, would poke his head through the broken panel and greet our commander with, "Hello Assassin," an endearing term he liked to use. Champ was an intellectual type, a West Point grad just like Woody, my flight commander. It seemed like all those 'Hudson High' types had neat little terms they liked to use and 'assassin' was his. Champ, however, was a solid troop, and he was happy for us to acquire our own phone so his flight troops didn't have to keep calling us when we had a call come in. Now it just so happened that someone fell heir to a field phone (I think it was a midnight requisition), the kind that has a canvas carrier with a crank on the side. And miraculously, it had just enough wire so it could be connected to the phone in "B" Flight. Champ and his troops were all for this if we agreed to answer half of the incoming calls. It was a deal. "A" Flight was in the phone business.

To celebrate this great acquisition, we threw a party. Little excuse was needed to have a party, but every little occasion was never left to chance. Things were going along at a great pace when someone suggested we call San Antonio on the new phone! Why San Antonio, I don't know, but it was as good a place as any; someone must have had an old and dear friend there. To get to San Antonio by phone from Korea wasn't the easiest of tasks. You had to go through several operators, the first of which was Comet Forward (the call sign for the Seoul telephone exchange), then on to Comet Rear (Pusan exchange which was still in Korea), Tokyo (everything went through Tokyo), San Francisco (finally across the big pond), and then if luck held, San Antonio. It might be a large undertaking since going through that many switchboards would create a lot of line drop or energy loss, but with all the juice (booze) we had in us, we were willing to try anything.

A quick twist of the crank and a little ring, ring, ring got us the Comet Forward operator, "Comet Forward, give us Comet Rear." Just a whisper was required as Comet Forward was just over the ridge. Almost immediately we heard the Comet Rear operator, "Comet Rear, give us Tokyo." A little more volume now as we progressed up the line, and the time between receiving operators began to lengthen, "Tokyo, give us.. **San Francisco.**" The volume was beginning to get into the higher decibel levels, and heads were beginning to turn to see what was going on. 'Quiet guys, we are about to get through to Frisco'! **"San Francisco, give us San Antonio"**.. "mumble, mumble, mumble".. was that the Frisco operator? **"San Fran.. how do you read me?."** "Mumble, snap, Who is calling San Francisco?"........ **"I say again, San Francisco, give us San Antonio"**...."Calling San Fran"........**"I say, San Francisco, give us San Antonio"**...... Things went dead, and nothing was happening now except for a lot of crackling noise on the line. We were hoarse, we were worn down, we couldn't even hear a recognizable sound, much less an operator's voice. The party had come to a standstill with everyone huddled around this fine invention of Graham Bell's. (He would have probably rolled over in his grave if he could have seen what we were doing with his brain child). Immediately interest was lost in the call; we couldn't even find the troop who had wanted to call San Antonio (?) in the first place, so back to the party while there was still booze to be consumed!

Well, we didn't make it through to San Antonio, but at least we heard San Francisco. Boy, "A" Flight was really coming up in the world. This year overseas telephone service, maybe next year indoor water? There was a suggestion that we might want to switch to semaphore or smoke signals before we tried again, but with only 100 missions to fly and nobody we really knew in San Antonio anyway, who really cared?

13

"Round Trip to Tokyo"

My missions had been completed and my orders had been screwed up for my return to the States. For how long, I wasn't sure, but if I didn't get my flying time for December, I wasn't going to get the much needed flying pay. Combat was out, but I had volunteered for any test flights or ferry missions that might come up. It just so happened that in early December the Wing Commander had taken some hits from a Mig on his last mission, and the plane couldn't be repaired locally. Someone was needed to take it back to Yokota Air Base in Japan for a complete overhaul. Yokota was just on the outskirts of Tokyo, now that wouldn't be a bad deal at all. It would also mean a new F-86 must be picked up at the port and flown south to be made ready for combat. At the replacement depot, another aircraft would be ready for either the 51st Wing at Suwon or for the 4th at Kimpo. Either way, the round trip would insure the required flying time for the month. Best get it now in case my new orders arrived early, I should be so lucky.

It must have been 0' early something in the morning on a very gray and gloomy day. The night before had been a typical party evening for us combat veterans with no reason to arise at a normal hour. Sooooo... the loud ringing of the telephone was very disturbing and piercing to my tender ears. Who would have the audacity to shatter the peace and tranquillity of the day. I snatched the phone up and said, "Hello, can I help you destroy the base or some other world landmark?" I wasn't at my best when first aroused. "Lieutenant, thought you were going to take this bird back to Japan for us(?)," blasted our line chief's voice. Oh yes, I had said I would do something along that line in the near future, that future must be now! As I was trying to clear the old head bone I glanced out the window and it was snowing. "My God chief, it's snowing outside," I said in defense of my tardiness. "What does that have to do with flying? We need to get this thing out of the hangar. Are you going to take it or not?" Man, he was persistent. "OK, OK, I'll be there in about twenty minutes. Be sure I've got full tanks, I don't want to have to stop short."

It was like being in a fog, trying to get a few things together for the trip plus insure I had some idea of exactly where I was going in the first place. After about fifteen minutes of stumbling and getting shaved and showered, I was out the door and on my way to the flight line. Five minutes to file a flight plan and I was at the hangar with my chute and helmet. Ye gads! The sabre was covered with snow. "No sweat," said the Chief, "it will blow off on take-off." Easy for you to say Sarge, I thought, he didn't have to take this monster up into this gray cruel day. Oh well, let's get on with it. I climbed up into the cockpit and settled down into the seat. As I looked around, I couldn't see out! HELP, I'M BLIND? Whee, it was OK, I had just gone all the way to the bottom of the seat, there was no dinghy pack in place that normally functioned as the seat cushion. "Sarge, I need a dinghy pack." "Sorry sir, no extras, only the ones for the combat birds." As he spoke he was holding a small drink bottle crate, "This will have to do," he said with a slight grin that spelled, 'Don't be late for take-off again.' Great, if I had to eject, it would require weeks just to get the splinters out of my ass.

I was finally airborne, into the gray snow clogged murk that made up the major portion of the horizon for that day. It really didn't matter much, the drink crate didn't give me the height I was normally used to, so I just stared directly at the instrument panel and headed for the Land of the Rising Sun. Finally I reached the top of the overcast and saw my first sunlight of the day. It was nice up there, screne and quite, only the puffy tops of the clouds below, looking like a vast lake of milk which stretched as far as the eye could see. I was on course and making all the checkpoints on time. Was I really halfway across the Sea of Japan by now? Why was the left wing so heavy? Wonder if these clouds went all the way to Tokyo? Lots of questions when there was no one to talk with. Hell, that left wing is heavy, I think my left external fuel tank didn't feed. Now that presented a real problem, without that fuel, getting to the Tokyo area was an 'iffy' proposition. For sure, dragging that full tank along would make it impossible. It hadn't been any big thing to expend tanks when flying combat, but here over an international waterway, there could be some difficulty. What was under the clouds below? Maybe I would hit a ship or something? Maybe there were small islands with people living on them? How was I going to make it to a suitable landing place still carrying that full tank? Zing.........Zap! My finger stabbed the tank jettison button without the least bit of hesitation. Screw those ships and people!

Now fuel was the most critical item on board. The clouds were still below and it looked like they went all the way

43

to the North Pole. Weather confirmed that when I asked for an update. Getting to Yokota was not in the cards tonight, I'll just stop by Nagoya for 'Happy Hour.'

When I arrived over the Nagoya beacon, the sun was slowly sinking into the cloudy western sky. The fuel gage said it was time to get this ship on the ground and I was ready for a small libation, it had been a long day. Nagoya Control cleared me for an unrestricted letdown, so as soon as I crossed the beacon I cut power and descended into the murk. Suddenly it got very dark, I could barely see the instrument panel. The cockpit lighting appeared to be inoperable and my flashlight was back at Kimpo in my footlocker. Raising my sun visor helped a little, but between no lights and the low fuel state, landing was not only desirable, but mandatory.

I broke out of the clouds about two thousand feet above the ground. I could see the runway and lost no time in turning initial approach. I made a smart pitchout, and was on base leg with the gear on its way down. I was just ready to call 'gear down and locked' when the right main gear light didn't indicate a safe condition. GREAT! I quickly called the tower and said I would come by for a visual check, it had felt like all three gear had snapped down, but who could be sure. The tower operator said, "Sir, I will call the Airdrome Officer up to the tower to check your gear, I can't provide that information." Boulder Dash! Heifer Dust! I couldn't wait that long. "Tower, if I have to wait for him, he will be needed at my crash site." Then very calmly I said, "TELL ME IF YOU SEE THREE THINGS HANGING DOWN." As I flashed by he said, "Yes."

I made it to the parking area with pints of fuel to spare, also if it hadn't been for the lighting on the ramp, I would've required a seeing eye dog to find it. Lead me to the bar!

The next morning dawned loud and clear, the flight to Yokota was a piece of cake. The gear still didn't show down and locked, but that was to be expected. I wrote the discrepancies down for them including the lights, etal, and was off to town.

Twelve hot baths later, I gathered my prune wrinkled body and started the trip back to Kimpo. It was totally uneventful. After the flight over, I deserved a rest from the great unknown. A quick flight with a brand new Sabre from the port to the depot. Then the last leg from southern Japan to the home drome, completed the time required to earn my flying pay.

It had been eight days since I said farewell to our line chief, I wonder if he would remember me? As I pulled into the squadron parking area, and shut down the engine, the first words out of his mouth were, "Where is my drink bottle crate?" "I traded it for a Hot Bath! Thanks Chief, it made my whole week." He smiled and said, "From the way you looked when you departed, you probably needed more than one." If he only knew!

Now...what to do for the rest of the month?

1 4

"The Key is Pin Point Accuracy"

As I said, I knew things were messed up when my last missions were running down and I still didn't have my next assignment. It was particularly upsetting that they mixed up my orders, which meant that I would be in Korea for an extra month without getting to fly combat. If it hadn't been for that trip back to Tokyo early in the waiting period, I may have really gone off the deep end. December, the coldest and most unpleasant month of them all, made it doubly disagreeable. Well, that's what happened and I was really torqued about it! That left the rest of the time after the Tokyo episode with nothing to do but eat and drink. As it turned out, there seemed to be a heavier emphasis on drinking for the portion of the time I had left to kill. Looking back on the experience, which is a little hazy, there were two moments that will always be remembered. Maybe it was the shock effect that etched them in my memory. Anyway each incident surely got my attention.

***

One hazy night, both brain and weather wise, I was weaving my way back to my small nook in that great expanse called Kimpo. I decided that it was too early for bed, so I would stop in and check on my good old buddies in "C" Flight. They were always ready for a few laughs and a short nip or two, plus I could still see their light on so I knew they were still open for visitors. However, on this evening, things were a bit different from the ones I had remembered in the past. As I entered the flight room door, I was greeted with a barrage of gunfire. Bullets were literally flying around the cement interior of their flight room for what appeared to be unexplainable reasons. I am not sure where the ricochets were going, but it was a Zing here and a Zing there and a few seemed to whiz very near my head. I could have used a steel helmet or at least a flack vest. Having neither, I just ducked. What really made it a strange situation was when I realized that everyone was in the sack, and all were attempting to zero in on the lone light bulb hanging from the ceiling. It seemed that no one wanted to get out of bed to turn out the light, so they were doing their best to shoot it out. Such brilliant minds almost floored me; actually they almost shot me! I wasn't at my quickest, but it slowly dawned on me that this type of sport could be hazardous to one's health, either in bed or just by being inside the room. After what seemed like a millennium and while they were reloading, I sprang into action and hurled my half empty glass of bourbon and branch water in the direction of the bulb. Miraculously, I scored a direct hit. The sudden darkness was like an instant cease-fire and was greeted with sighs of relief, one snore, and a "Thanks a lot, Dan, come back earlier tomorrow night."

I guess I had just missed their Happy Hour? I could almost see the headlines, 'Young fighter pilot shot down in squadron flight quarters after completing 100 combat missions. He came between his squadron mates and a light bulb.' Ugh! I was certain that I wanted to stop by their place a lot earlier the next time!

***

The other memorable evening occurred as I was returning to my bunk on a freezing night just prior to the completion of my month of agony. I was proceeding down the loose brick walkway between the flight room buildings of the 334th and 335th Fighter Squadrons when the sounds of a party came drifting from one of the flight windows of the 334th. It must have been a hot time, for you really didn't need the windows open on this sub-zero night. As I came abeam of the window, I was hailed over with, "We are having a survey to see if......" then when I got to the window, "....water is ...WET?" Without warning, a bucket full of water was thrown in my face! Not a very nice gesture toward a veteran plodding through the cold night on his way to get a bit of sleep.

Now at sub-zero temperatures, that cold shot in the face really got my attention, so much so that for a moment it was difficult to get my breath. It seemed that some of the water froze when it hit the ground, or it should have at that temperature. I staggered back from the shock, almost tripping on the loose brick walkway. Instinctively, I reached down and picked up a brick; there had to be some retaliation. I hurled that brick straight for their window, saying, "I want to know if brick...... breaks GLASS?" Well, as luck would have it, the brick hit the four paned window squarely on the apex, where all four joined at the center. BULL'S EYE, a four for one shot. There was no glass left in that flight room's window, and they could count on some really fresh air, at least for the rest of that night. I don't know why they didn't invite me in?

We felt that some startling theories had been proven on this night, "Don't get between a Man and his Light Bulb," and "Water and Bricks not mixing," being the two main ones.

Needless to say, there was great celebration and consternation when I finally departed Kimpo. The 334th didn't have to worry about me during their late night parties, and "C" Flight would now have to get up and turn out their own light. However, I was certainly the most appreciative for finally getting on that stateside plane. I had made it through a 100 mission tour without a scratch, but even more miraculously, I had survived 30 evenings of late night Kimpo! To this day, I still don't know which was the more hair-raising.

Base Ops at Kimpo After Rehab

Sabres on the Ready at Kimpo

A Flight's Social and Reading Club. It Beat Bridge.

Woody and the Hot End of a Sabre

"Anyone for Bridge?" or "Gee, the Service in this Joint is Lousy."

THIS IS TO CERTIFY,

THAT Lt. DAN DRUEN

IS A BONA FIDE MEMBER OF THE

SIX O'CLOCK CLUB

AND IS ACTIVELY ENGAGED IN UPHOLDING

THE TRADITIONS OF THIS SACRED ORGANIZATION

PRESIDENT

SECRETARY

VICE PRESIDENT

Entry Level Certificate for Air Combat in Korea

USAF Fighter Weapons School Circa 1954-55. Big John was our Leader.

Godfrey Faster Than Sound

Cast of Thousands for Fire Power Demos During '58 Gunnery Meet at Nellis

Buckshot with Just a Few of the Trophies

The Front End of a Super Sabre. Pilot Posing for a
Jump Start.

Line-Up of Suspected Rustlers. Back Row Troops are
Two Time Losers.

Fighter Weapons School F-100's with Sunrise Mountain
in Background. Ski Resort on Sunrise Not Yet Open.

510th F-100 Taxiing for Take Off. Local Sheriff Looking for his Horse.

Big Mike Being Guarded for Not Counting to '3' Properly. A Thousand and One, A Thousand and Two...

One Super Party Coordinator

A Toast to the Aussies

"Tower, My Wingman Can't See Any Cable Dragging."

"Another Perfect Landing by the Purple Tailed Hawks"

Part Two

NELLIS

In the fifties, Nellis Air Force Base (AFB), in Las Vegas, Nevada, was one of two mainstay combat crew training bases. The other, Luke AFB, was near Phoenix, Arizona. Luke provided the upgrading and gunnery training for the Republic F-84 Thunderjet. Nellis, specialized their training utilizing the North American F-86 Sabrejet and the F-100 Super Sabre. Scores of new and old fighter pilots passed through the Nellis training squadrons. There were five squadrons that were strictly combat crew training units and one, the USAF Fighter Weapons School. It provided the graduate course for the fighter world. These stories attempt to relate some of the more amusing instances that occurred during those early days. They are also about a few of those pilots who made up that vast group of super jocks.

1 5

"A Salute to Armed Forces Day"

The day was clear and bright, not a cloud in the sky. It was early in the morning with barely more than a few souls stirring. It was a Holiday! The 3525th Aircraft Gunnery Squadron, also known as the Air Force Fighter Weapons School, had the job of performing the Armed Forces Day fly-by. Since it was a Saturday, it wasn't really such an honor, everybody else had the day off. Maybe we were being punished for something, or it was just our turn in the barrel? At least we were going to have an early take-off, that way the entire day wouldn't be shot. The plan called for sixteen F-86's to make a pass over Boulder City, then proceed down the length of Fremont Street (the heart of downtown Las Vegas), finishing with several passes along the Strip (location of the more glamorous hotels in Vegas). Big John G., our squadron commander, was to lead this gaggle. He was a giant of a man, somewhere between Superman and John Wayne. He could have been a middle linebacker for any pro team of the day, but his chosen profession was the fighter air force and he was excellent at his work. Checker, for the checker markings on the tails of the squadron's aircraft, was the lead flight's call sign. Red, White, and Blue followed for the second, third, and fourth flights. How patriotic can one be? I was Green sixteen or the last guy in the last flight. Actually, my call sign was Blue Four, but in that size of a gaggle, tailend Charlie was always known as 'Green sixteen.'

As mentioned earlier, it was a beautiful day in the Las Vegas valley. The visibility was listed as 35 miles, but with a little altitude, you could almost see downtown Los Angeles, (well maybe only Barstow), but it sure was crystal clear. The air even smelled good, it seemed to give an extra spring to each step and added emphasis to just being alive.

The briefing was short and sweet, put the light on the star and don't call unless you see fire. We would take-off in two ship elements and join into flights of four. Each flight would have the second element join to the right of the leader which made a normal finger-tip formation, just like looking at the four fingers on your right hand. Flights would be in trail, which meant that the last flight would be stacked down about five hundred feet lower than the leader.

The join-up went smoothly and before anyone was aware of it, we were squared away over Lake Mead and ready for our pass over Boulder City. Lead brought the flight in over Hoover Dam, which is just east of the town, at minimum altitude. There are many, many high voltage towers that surround the area, but somehow we managed to either go between them or around them. (I'm almost sure we didn't go under any of them). Before you could say 'Whoops,' we were turning to follow the highway into Vegas. This required a fairly sharp turn through Railroad Pass which put old 'Green 16' looking straight up at my flight leader as we went through the pass. It was like being on the tail-end of a crack-the-whip game. When the leader banks about 20 degrees to line up for the proper course, tail-end Charlie gets to quadruple it which equated to being very close to a 90 degree bank. Wheee! Were we having fun yet?

In the fifties, the buildings on Fremont Street were only two stories high, in fact, there wasn't anything in town that was more than three with the exception of a few of the gaudy signs both downtown and on the strip. As checker lead started down Fremont he said, "Blue four, tell me when we are low enough." It wasn't long before I said, "Hold it there lead, I'm looking into hotel windows now!" That put us at minimum altitude as we cruised from east to west along 'Glitter Gulch.' There must have been a few people that heard us coming and staggered out of the bars and gaming establishments to see just what the H— was going on. But before any of them could get a glimpse, we had streaked by, and were making a long left turn to hit the Strip. The only thing I remember as we went swishing down between the neon signs was Vegas Vic (the tallest sign on Fremont Street in those days) and I looking eyeball to eyeball. The sign's arm moves back and forth and has been one of the trademarks of Las Vegas for many years. Luckily I was on the right side of the street and Vegas Vic was on the left or he might have 'goosed' me as we went by. Checker lead wasn't giving us anything to spare. A bit lower and I could have pulled a few slot handles myself.

We zipped the length of the Strip, both down and back so we wouldn't miss any of the plush resorts. Our 'Ground Zero' on the Strip was the Desert Inn golf course. Lead called for each flight to break off individually and to make passes at various corners of the course. He wanted all those dear souls to remember what Armed Forces Day was all about. After approximately five minutes of simulated attacks, the following radio transmission was heard. "Checker Lead, this is Nellis tower. We are receiving a few phone calls concerning some low flying aircraft in the area of the Strip." (Imagine that!) It must be that some of the early morning gamblers were being disturbed by swooshing noises from somewhere outside. Also, the fact that traffic had slowed to a stop on the Strip couldn't have had anything to do with such complaints.

"Tower, Checker lead, tell them they are lucky we aren't using REAL BULLETS." And we continued to harass the few golfers that were up that early in the morning.

There seemed to be a calm in the air after that air clearing statement. Lead rejoined the four flights in the initial trail formation for one last pass down Fremont Street before returning to the base. This time he was planning to go from west to east. Uh-oh! Vegas Vic and I were going to be on the same side of the street. As we flashed over the casinos for this last pass, I could've sworn something tickled the bottom of my aircraft. Probably just my imagination.

To my knowledge, nothing adverse was ever heard about our 'airshow,' I guess those phone calls were really from the five percent that don't like anything. There must have been more patriots down there than we realized. Hurray for flying, gambling, the red, white, and blue, and the patriotic people of Las Vegas.

May Old Glory and Vegas Vic always wave!

16

"Free Advice for Sale"

While the primary mission at Nellis AFB in the mid-50's was to train new fighter pilots in the skills of air-to-ground and air-to-air gunnery, each flying unit had a back-up requirement to augment the Air Defense forces on the West Coast. Each squadron had a designated base, which they would deploy to in the event of an emergency alert condition. This was the Air Force's way of justifying the number of aircraft that were used in their advanced training schools. It also gave the trainers a way to keep up on the latest air defense tactics and procedures. Periodically, each unit would make a practice deployment to insure they knew just where and how they would operate. Due to the size of the Fighter Weapons School, which was the advanced gunnery school that produced fighter gunnery instructors, two bases were assigned, thus requiring the squadron to separate into two air defense detachments for deployments.

The initial unit from the Weapons School was led by the squadron commander, Big John, and the squadron operations officer was his number two man. Their deployment base was Hamilton AFB, just North of the San Francisco Bay Bridge. It was an ideal place for a practice deployment. San Francisco was only several minutes away, and practice deployments didn't require flying every second of the day. There was time to visit the sights and take part in the sounds of the City by the Bay. Needless to say, being a member of the initial unit was one of the best deals in town—that is, if you liked San Francisco. Big John certainly did, and so did almost everyone else in the squadron. At least half the outfit was happy!

Now the second unit was not quite that fortunate. They were assigned to McClellan AFB in the fair town of Sacramento. This is not to say that Sacramento wasn't a swinging place, but it didn't quite stand up to the Bay Area in many people's minds (the other half of the squadron). The second unit was headed by a gung-ho pilot named Ray L. I had the stroke of luck(?) to be his operations officer even though I was somewhat junior in rank to other jocks in the squadron. That ought to tell you something! Ray was not the shy type in any sense of the word and had no trouble defying military tradition. He was as outgoing as anyone could get. He liked to mingle with the crowd and was always a part of any scene, whether he had been invited or not. Since it fell our lot to be in charge, it was also our responsibility to make inspection visits to the location. We had to insure that all was in readiness if, and when, we were required to deploy. One such trip still stands out in my mind.

The weather wasn't supposed to be as bad as it turned out to be, but here we were on a ground control approach (GCA) to McClellan AFB, at night, with the weather just above the minimums allowable for landing. We had taken two F-86's without external fuel tanks. Ray insisted that the flight was such a short one, there was no need for the ground crew to trouble themselves with tank installation. I really wished we had put them to the trouble, for we were now on GCA with the barest amount of gas. Despite having a bit of radio trouble to compound the problem, we made the approach and landed without major mishap. Ray thought it was routine. I thought he was mad, and I was out of my mind to be following this wild maniac.

We had arrived too late to worry about the base. We had all the next day to see about our operations set-up. There was no need to accomplish all of our business in one stroke, so we were off to town to the nearest bar. I didn't know about Ray's nerves, but mine were a bit ragged from the trip over from Nellis, particularly the last part. It didn't take long to arrive at a very refined and crowded establishment that served alcoholic beverages. As we edged our way in, trying to find a place at a very crowded bar, I was able to reach over and order the drinks. Ray, in the meantime, got into a conversation with a drunk who had just been cut off by the bartender. The drunk wasn't causing any problems; he was just standing peaceably against the wall minding his own business. He was a bit upset that he couldn't get another drink and was willing to let anyone know that would give him the time. Ray was the perfect sympathizer, a Mr. 'I'll Help You Out of Your Troubles' personified.

As I turned back to where Ray and the drunk were standing, Ray was saying, "I wouldn't let anyone do that to me!" The drunk's eyes were glazed, but he was hanging on every word Ray was saying. "No sir, no bartender would ever tell me I couldn't have a drink!" A slurred "Mmmmm" was the reply. "Yeah," Ray continued, "do you know what I would do if that was tried on me?" A lolling shake of the head indicated that he didn't know. "Well, I would reach over that bar and

66

grab that bartender by the tie. I would pull him halfway across the bar and say, 'Give me a drink or I will drag you all the way over this bar.' That's what I would do." The drunk nodded and moved slowly away, presumably to get more advice from someone else.

Ray and I finally got our drinks and were looking the place over when suddenly both bartenders leaped over the bar and were literally throwing the old drunk out the front door. The drunk was hanging on for dear life to the tie of the largest and toughest looking bartender.

Ray, in his casual manner, turned to me and said, "I wonder what happened to him?" I was stunned, "WHAT HAPPENED TO HIM, what do you mean, HAPPENED to him? You just got him thrown out of the bar!" My comment just rolled over his head like water off of a duck's back. Ray said, "Gee, I didn't think the old man was that crazy. He should have at least grabbed the little one's tie!"

1 7

"Was It Really a UFO?"

Nifty McCrystal was well known for his varied escapades, one of which was related in an earlier chapter. Remember, he was that interesting individual who gave that Mig pilot those big round eyes. There are many other stories about Nifty, but probably the most widely renowned, was a situation that occurred on his way back from a Florida trip.

It was a cloudy and rainy night when Nifty was winging his way back to Nellis AFB in Las Vegas, Nevada. His first stop was scheduled for Barksdale AFB in Shreveport, Louisiana. Barksdale was a Strategic Air Command (SAC) base well known for its tough security measures. They were responsible for the nation's nuclear forces, and they weren't about to let just anybody land at their bases without insuring that they had a right to be there. Nifty had filed a proper flight plan, so by all standards he was legal and expected to be stopping for fuel. But when a visiting aircraft was stopping at a SAC base at night, it was sure to be greeted by the SAC Security Police, legal or not. It is said that they overplayed their roles sometimes just to insure the impression they were really on their toes. It must be said they were experts at their job. They played their parts to the hilt. This was nothing really new to Nifty though, he had been slightly harassed before, so this time he really wanted to make them earn their money.

Nifty was flying alone in a tandem-seated T-33 and had his luggauge stored in the empty backseat. Between the two cockpits, he had placed a very large goldfish bowl that wouldn't fit in the rear seat. He was being very careful so that he wouldn't break the goldfish bowl since it was a present for his wife. He was right on his Expected Time of Arrival (ETA). He made the proper and prescribed approach and executed the smoothest of landings. He taxied up to a rain slick ramp, only to be met by two security police trucks full of cops who had their guns and bright lights trained directly on Nifty's cockpit. Nifty was not about to be intimidated by such brazen tactics. As soon as he opened the canopy, he quickly took his flying helmet off, reached around and put the goldfish bowl over his head. You can imagine what bright lights reflecting on a rain spotted goldfish bowl might look like. It was like something

68

out of Space Digest, and Nifty was taking full advantage of it. The Air Policemen (AP's) were confused, looking up at what appeared to be a large glowing head with wild looking eyes and a sadistic mouth. Nifty was at his best. Slowly he surveyed the area, finally bringing his focus to the group at the foot of the aircraft ladder. Speaking slowly and a bit marble mouthed, he said, "I'm from Planet X. Take me to your leader. There are more to follow!" Before they could drag him from the cockpit, Nifty climbed down, remaining aloof and firm.

They certainly thought he was kidding. What kind of nut was this on such a miserable night? But Nifty was sticking to his story. He walked a little stiff legged with his arms at slight angles away from his body, swaying as he moved away from the T-33. As they approached him, he stopped, holding his arms out wide, and said again, "I'm from Planet X. Take me to your leader. There are more to follow!" Well the AP's weren't about to put up with this malarkey for long, so they hauled him off to their Command Center.

Now the Base Commander, who was asleep, was going to have to be awakened so he could deal with this nutcake. The AP's were wet, tired and not getting paid to deal with this sort. They really didn't want to have to wake the Colonel, but there seemed to be no other alternative. Nifty wasn't making it any easier on them. He was playing his part to the hilt. He would mumble a few incoherent words, roll his eyes around and hum a few bars of the Star Trek theme. Oh! I forgot to mention that it was 0100 hours, which is 1 in the morning. You can understand how disgruntled the Base Commander felt about being awakened, particularly at that early morning hour. He had no earthly desire to go down and talk to some fighter jock who was creating a disturbance for his people and his base.

Nifty was enjoying the entire thing, having a hot cup of coffee, keeping dry and busily drying off his outer-space helmet (his goldfish bowl). About that time, in walked the Base Commander, and he really wasn't in the best of moods. Nifty stood up to attention and started to say, "I'm fro......." when the Base Commander loudly interrupted and said, "Get your damned goldfish bowl, your silly little airplane, and get off of this G.D. base. If I ever see you here again, I will put you under the jail, and *your leaders* will have a hard time ever finding you. Is that clear?"

Nifty didn't have to be told twice. He dashed to his bird, stowed his goldfish bowl, and started his engine. Just prior to taxi out for take-off, according to Nifty, "I cocked the nose wheel, did two quick 360 degree turns at full throttle. I dusted them off just to show them they hadn't scared me. Although, I didn't really feel relieved until I was airborne and into that dark pleasant cloak of night."

Just for the record, I don't believe Nifty ever visited Barksdale AFB again. In fact, he was heard to say, "I'm blanking out the entire state of Louisiana from my cross-country map. I'm not sure that I would be welcome there any more!"

"Vertigo on a Major Scale"

During the early 1950's, about '53 or '54, the Air Force started to replace the F-84's in Europe with F-86's. Naturally the Ferry Command didn't have enough Sabre pilots to make such a mass move, so they had to call on other resources to make the exchange. Nellis AFB was an ideal place in those days to get the necessary manpower. It was blessed with the majority of the qualified F-86 pilots in the Air Force at that time. Most of these were bachelors who were more than happy to have an expense paid trip to Europe. The trip called for a pick-up of the aircraft in Charleston, S.C.; then on to Dover, Del.; Presque Isle, Maine; Goose Bay, Labrador; BW-1, Greenland; Keflavik, Iceland; Preswick, Scotland; and then to a designated base in Germany. The return trip was made by Material Airlift Command (MAC) or commercial carrier. If the pilots were lucky enough to come back commercial, they might get to stop in Paris. So there was a lot of incentive for the trip, and there wasn't any trouble getting the number required for each flight. It took the best part of two or three weeks to complete the trip, and that was if the weather didn't sock them in at one of the stops. Such was the case in the trip that Bill L. and Mike made. Bill L. was tall and rangy. He had only been at Nellis a short time, so he was happy to be selected so early for this great trip. Mike was an old friend. He was from the flat lands of Iowa, and had been in the flying school class just behind mine. He was as good a fighter pilot as you could come by.

Everything was going great. The aircraft pick-up had gone according to plan. The stopovers at Dover and Presque Isle were a breeze, the sun was shinning and Germany and Paris were only a few days away. Then they arrived in Goose Bay. The weather gods suddenly became a major factor. The skies clouded and the forecast was for heavy snow and lots of it. For once the weather guessers hit it dead on the nose. It started snowing and appeared it would never stop. Entire operations on the base were brought to a standstill. But of paramount importance to Bill and Mike, their gaggle was stranded in the snowy confines of Goose Bay for almost a week. Luckily, Goose Bay had an Officers Club, a fair size cadre of nurses, and enough food and drink to last for weeks on end. This meant there was companionship and the substances required to sustain life. Now any red blooded young fighter pilot can take these three ingredients and survive longer than the average individual. Our troops were in a survival situation that they could handle.

On this particular evening, Bill and Mike had been in the company of two very nice nurses. They had spent the evening eating, drinking and dancing at the Officers Club. Bill had borrowed a car from a local troop, so transport wasn't a problem, provided they could navigate on the snow-covered roadways. That wasn't a problem either since Bill was from the sun kissed lands of North Dakota. He didn't even know roads were covered with anything else but snow until he departed for the Air Force. The two couples had a splendid evening and danced and partied until the wee hours of the morning.

They had delivered the two young ladies back to their billets and were on their way back to the Visiting Officers Quarters (VOQ) with Bill at the wheel. It turned out to be one of the snowiest nights in Goose Bays' history—a "5 Star Blizzard." Naturally our two intrepid airmen had put a little of the sour mash away, and they were not about to get into trouble with the gendarme, so Bill was at Warp Creep. In fact, they were proceeding at barely 5 MPH in a complete white-out. It was difficult to see even inches in front of the car. Bill was hunched over the steering wheel, carefully making his way along a difficult thoroughfare, intent only on arriving back at the VOQ in a safe and uncompromised (arrested) condition. Mike was half asleep.

Bill continued to inch slowly down the road, peering into a white sea of snow when there came a tapping at the driver's side window. Tap, tap, tap! Bill tried to ignored it as he looked from the speedometer to the window and back again. Surely there must be some mistake. Who in the world could be outside tapping at his window while he was driving down the road trying so desperately to get back to the haven and safety of the VOQ? But again—tap, tap, tap—becoming more persistent by the moment. It couldn't be ignored much longer, and it sure was playing havoc with Bill's concentration while he was driving. Finally, Bill lowered his window, never deviating from his stalwart task. Even Mike thought the condition odd, but he didn't want to add any more confusion to an already amazing situation.

Standing there, perfectly still, was an Air Policeman. Bill immediately rolled the window back up and tried to ignore what he had just witnessed and at the same time, conquer his vertigo. Can you imagine the impact of speeding along and having a body standing at rest just outside your window? He was proceeding home, minding his own business at 5MPH, and some clown was standing dead still outside his world. By now, the tapping had reached a very persistent level and could not be ignored for another second. His vertigo had completely engulfed him, so in utter frustration, he lowered the window and moved the gear lever to neutral. He was totally disgusted. The very nice young Air Policeman standing by the window wanted to know if he could give them a lift back to the VOQ? Since ..... 'their car had gone head first into a snow bank, burying itself up to the hood; the back wheels were in a smooth rut, slowly ticking over at 5 MPH; and the windshield wipers were grudgingly moving the snow back and forth on the windshield'.

Such was life on a winter's night in far off Labrador! Tomorrow the sun would shine, and maybe this whole affair would turn out to be just a bad dream—NOT!

"Patuxent River Naval Air Station Never Looked So Good"

Everyone at Nellis Air Force Base (AFB), in Las Vegas, Nevada, had their name on the "High Flight" volunteer list. These coveted missions, shuttled F-86's from the United States to Europe. They were usually very routine and highly desirable, a real 'boondoggle.' Several of us had been on the volunteer list for months. However, it was just by chance that 'Red Dog,' my operations officer, Jerry, a free spirit, and I were selected for the same deployment. Jerry was your basic tried and true fighter pilot. He had tangled with his share of Migs in the skies over North Korea, and done well. Red Dog was a legend in his own time. He had a direct approach to any situation that went right to the heart of the problem. A six foot two tower of rare bone fighter man. There was never doubt in your mind after Red Dog provided his input. The three of us were the only ones from Nellis on this particular shuttle flight. Even more coincidental was that we made up the last three aircraft cell in the overall nineteen ship movement. There were four flights of four aircraft, and us. Bringing up the rear.

Most of the flights were led by Ferry Command pilots who did nothing but make these trips. Supposedly, they were 'expert' in all the rules and regulations required when flying military aircraft across the great Atlantic expanse. Such was the case for the first four flights, but since the last three aircraft had been add-ons, Red Dog was allowed to lead this three ship element. The fact that he had more F-86 flight time than the other four leaders combined, was of no consequence. The powers-to-be were reluctant to break precedence, but in this case they had no choice. They were flat out of Ferry Command types.

The first leg of the route went from Charleston, South Carolina to Dover AFB, Delaware. No big step for a climber, a mere 520 miles or so. Probably no more than one hour and twenty minutes in an F-86. Any experienced fighter pilot with tons of flying time could make that flight in his sleep. These ferry people weren't dealing with kids, get serious.

The pre-flight details had been completed. That included: flight testing the aircraft, survival suit fittings, and route planning. Tomorrow was launch day, but tonight was unwind time. A good meal, a couple of drinks, then off to the sack for an early get up. Flight briefing was 0600, or six o'clock, to those that are not familiar with the twenty-four hour clock system. Launch was nine!

The meal was delicious, the drinks relaxing, but Red Dog and Jerry decided their evening required more. So off to a near-by night spot for an additional night cap or two. After all, we were only going 500 or so miles tomorrow, a piece of cake! I declined their generous offer to accompany. As the junior ranking officer, I would get the crew rest for the three of us. Ugh!

The get-up time came early. I was pleased to see that Red Dog and Jerry were present for duty. I seemed to recall hearing their earlier arrival. Must have been well within crew rest requirements, so I didn't pay any attention to the hour. Rules were that you couldn't drink within, either eight feet of the aircraft, or eight hours before flight time. I never could remember which, must have been the footage rule! Anyway, the three of us were at the dawn briefing, raring to proceed to Dover.

Weather was a factor. Fifteen hundred foot ragged overcast, with some thunderstorms in the area. Visibility was good below the overcast, so there really shouldn't have been a problem. Our flight plan called for us to climb to thirty-five thousand feet, remain at that altitude for about twenty minutes, then make the let-down to Dover airpatch.

The first sixteen aircraft had blasted off into the murky sky. Flights of four were spaced fifteen minutes apart to allow for climb-out and instrument let-down separation. Our three sparkling Sabrejets took the runway fourteen minutes after the preceding flight. On the mark, we applied full power, roared down the runway, and soared into the gray sky of South Carolina. I was the number two man flying close wing-tip formation on Red Dog's right wing. Within seconds, Jerry was abroad, and into formation on Red Dog's left wing. Red Dog turned our three ships onto the departure course, and we were on our way.

Almost immediately we vanished into the overcast. We were in that gray mist that envelopes you, and everything it seems to touch. There was no bottom or top to your world. You could be up-side down, and never know the difference. There wasn't enough visibility to move into a looser formation, which is usually the case when going from point A to B in fair weather. However, the cockpit instruments could still be checked with an occasional glance away from the leader's wing-tip. They gave you some feeling for the proper attitude. We were climbing through twenty thousand feet with everything proceeding according to plan. External wing fuel tanks were feeding properly, and all engine instruments were in the green; normal. As we approached thirty thousand feet we began to pop in and out of the cloud tops. Higher clouds could be seen ahead on our course. These were the isolated thunderstorms we had heard about during our enroute weather briefing. No problem, just so long as we didn't get caught in their boiling, tumbling turbulence.

As we climbed through thirty-two thousand, Red Dog started to level the flight. Why? Our flight plan called for leveling at thirty-five thousand. "Lead," Jerry called, "I've got 32 on my gauge." "Yeah, so have I," came Red Dog's curt reply. "This is high enough for me. I don't intend to set any altitude records." Red Dog had a way with words. There wasn't even a microphone click in response to that edict. Maybe his late night sojourn was having some effect. Could be I was wrong on the crew rest rule. Maybe it *was,* eight *hours,* rather than the footage?

Not only did we level at thirty-two thousand, but we only stayed there for less than a couple of minutes. Here we were, almost immediately descending back into the clouds. As wingmen, we had no other choice but to move back into close formation, and hang-on. "Where are we headed lead?" I asked tentatively. "I think I see a hole ahead," came Red Dog's reply. "We will let down through it and miss those thunderstorms." That was wonderful logic but by my calculations we would be a bit short of our destination, if and when we broke out below the clouds. I was the low ranking aviator in this group, so I wasn't about to make any additional comments concerning my leader's plans.

It was a rough ride down through the murk, but finally we broke clear of the clouds. We were only about a thousand feet above the ground skimming along over flat marshes, someplace on the east coast of the United States. That estimated location was an assumption on my part. We had headed North from South Carolina, flown for about fifty minutes, then let down. At least we were far enough east to miss the Blue Ridge Mountains. Oh Boy, where to now?

There wasn't a recognizable land mark in sight. We went into spread formation, and immediately tried to tune-in

Dover radio. I think we must have each tuned-in a different thunderstorm. Nobody was able to obtain an accurate vector from their radio compass needle. "I think we may be a little South of Dover," was Red Dog's quizzical remark. 'A little South,' that was the understatement of the week. Before anyone could comment, the command to "Close-It-Up," crackled in our earphones. Back up into the murk we went. When we had first broken clear of the clouds our fuel state was adequate for another forty minutes or so. Of course, the longer we tooled around at low altitude, that time limit diminished drastically. So, the command to climb was welcomed, especially from the standpoint of finding a place to land before our fuel ran out.

At approximately eight thousand feet we hit a clear pocket in the clouds. Immediately, we loosened the formation, and tried to get our radio compasses to lock-in on any haven. Again, mixed results. "I think I have something, close-it-up," Red Dog commanded. No sooner accomplished, we were back in the clouds, and headed down.

Again, we broke clear at one thousand feet. Surprise, surprise! However, this time we found ourselves in some heavy rain. Also, our flight time remaining had been reduced to only a paltry ten or so minutes. I had bailed out of an F-86 one time before, in Korea. My engine had quit, but that is another story. Anyway, I was beginning to think that this might be the second time. There wasn't anything that even had a striking resemblance to an airport. The estuary complex below was dotted with a few palatial estates. (Maybe I could parachute near one of those? Funny, the thoughts that go through one's mind at a time like that.) We were spread as wide as the visibility would allow. We had turned North, then South, then North again in an attempt to spot a landing area. Nothing! My fuel gauge was beginning to bounce off "E." And that didn't stand for "Enough."

Suddenly to my left, we were headed South at the time, I caught a faint glimpse of a low, long gray area. "BREAK LEFT," I yelled, as if enemy aircraft were about to shoot us down. We spun around in a hard left turn. As we rolled out the gray area bloomed into a complex of runways, with a control tower and all the trimmings. Immediately, we attempted to make radio contact, but couldn't raise a soul for landing clearance. Regardless, it was a runway. We were on fumes. We were going to land, clearance or not!

The way we lined up, Jerry was first on the runway, Red Dog next, and I was tail-end Charlie. The runway had about a foot of water on it. Our touchdowns looked like three large mallards splashing down in the middle of the local duck pond. The spray we kicked up rivaled most motor boat races you've ever witnessed. As I rolled along on the runway, the water slowed me quickly to turn-off speed. To my right, I saw what looked like a Ground Control Approach (GCA) trailer. It was sitting on the runway, slightly towards the edge. Luckily it was just clear of the landing space we used. I was sure we weren't on the correct runway, or even an active one, but we certainly didn't care. It was pavement, and we were down safely. As Jerry cleared the runway, his engine flamed out. Red Dog made it halfway to the parking area before he coasted to a stop. I made it to the regular transient parking, with my fuel indicator below the "E" mark. The tower finally made contact on the 'Emergency' channel. However, by then, the situation had gone from, a high state of calm, to business as usual. The sign on the side of the control tower said, "Welcome to Patuxent River Naval Air Station." It never looked so good.

Meantime in the Dover Operations Center, the Ferry Command types were beginning to approach a panic stage. Where were their last three charges? Time had run out! No word, good or bad, had been received. They had never lost an aircraft before, much less three. As the story goes—"They are in Patuxent River," a sergeant manning the phone, said. "Oh my god!" came the exasperated voice of the mission leader. They say he went a ghostly white. However, before he dropped over in a dead faint, came—"Naval Air Station."

Of course the dynamic threesome weren't part of this loop. We knew where we were! We were busily getting our aircraft fueled and ready for the short dash from Patuxent NAS to Dover AFB. A short ninety miles or so, let's go low level. Whoopee, we hadn't tried that recently!

Needless to say, we weren't greeted as heroes upon our arrival on the Dover ramp. I'm not sure what the mission leader expected from Red Dog, but all he heard as Red Dog descended from the aircraft was, "See you at the bar!" His comment didn't leave room for a reply. So we made a stop at a Navy base, at least it was our Navy's!

Just another routine cross country flight. On to Europe! Watch out Royal Navy here we come. I could hardly wait!

20

"Night Flight to Denver"

The day had been very quiet for a Saturday. There had been a parade in the morning—but besides watching a few troops get medals for Korean action—plus all the units march (straggle—the Air Force wasn't meant to keep in step) by in review—it left the afternoon a total loss. There was the usual get together at the O'Club pool, but most of the bachelors went downtown or away from the base. The ones that lived in town, sacked out waiting for the bright lights to come on. Then would be the time to hit the strip and see what wondrous fantasies would occur. The female situation in Vegas wasn't the best. There were the show girls, but they worked into the wee hours of the new day, which wasn't conducive to flying airplanes in the pre-dawn hours of that same day. It was very difficult to meet locals or get acquainted with the out-of-town visitors. Both were really hit-or-miss propositions. Most of the single permanent party instructors relied on girls they met in some other towns or had known from way back when. One of our roommates had a case in point.

Bill W., an A-One aviator with excellent credentials from Korea, had met a stewardess with United when he was returning from one of the ferry trips to Europe. She often flew into Denver, but hardly ever got to Las Vegas. It had been a catch-as-catch-can relationship, very difficult for either of them to spend much time together. Sometimes he received a little advanced notice on her trips to Denver, other times it was a complete surprise. The later being the case on this waning Saturday afternoon.

Immediately after the parade, Bill, who was six one, one hundred and eighty pounds of good looking fighter pilot, had headed straight for one of those fabulous Saturday Champagne brunches. They were nearly exclusive to many of the Nellis fighter pilots. In reality, they were open to anyone who could drink at that time of day, and they were very reasonable which suited a young aviator's billfold. Bill had partaken heavily of the liquid portion of the brunch, so it was back to the pad for a nice afternoon nap before getting ready to hit the Strip with 'the gang'. Just as the sun was setting, the phone rang, stirring his slumber with a jolt. It was his 'Stew.'

She was in Denver, and was asking innocently—"Why can't you get an airplane and come on up!"

Little did she know about the Air Force and their weekly policy on cross-country flying. Requests must be submitted a week in advance, and approval wasn't always easy without a plan to accomplish a large amount of your annual flying requirements; such as letdowns, weather time, ground controlled approaches, and the like. But, he said, "I'll see what I can do." Now we were all in Red Dog's squadron, you may recall his forthright approach to living. He didn't mince words or leave any doubt in your mind on how he felt about you or any subject that you might bring up. It would be his call on getting an airplane at this late hour. It meant going to his quarters and asking him point blank. What was there to lose? Just your life—Red Dog could get violent!

"OK" was the surprising answer after he quizzed him on the brunch he knew he had attended. "We had a T-33 that Jake didn't take, try to get someone to go with you, I'll call maintenance to tell them you are coming down." What a surprise, Red Dog was almost civil, his only request was to try to get another troop to fill the back seat. That wasn't unreasonable. As Bill strolled through the O'Club with his helmet swinging lazily from his hand, he thought it odd that everyone was hiding behind the furniture to avoid his request. They must have known about the Brunch also! Well, he had tried, that's all Red Dog had demanded.

The two night maintenance people were alert and ready for Bill when he arrived at the flight line. In a matter of seconds he had stored his overnight bag and was fired up, ready to taxi. "Nellis tower, Tiger 698 ready for clearance, taxi, and takeoff," came Bill's crisp transmission. "Roger Tiger 698, you're cleared as filed, taxi to runway 19—you're number one for departure." The tower didn't have any other traffic, so Bill had a free rein. He didn't want to taxi all the way up to the North end of the field, so he said, "Tower, I'm headed North, how about Runway 01 for departure." Usually, when the wind wasn't a factor, night takeoffs were made towards the city lights of Las Vegas to allow for a horizon, to the North was nothing but a black hole. After a slight pause, a very questioning voice said, "Pilot's............Discretion."

It was only a matter of seconds before Bill was thundering down Runway 01. The runway boundary lights were flashing by with increasing speed. The plane became airborne at the computed distance, the last of the lights zipped by, and—Uh oh!—Everything turned black!—Where did the world go? Bill had expected some semblance of a horizon to aid in making a visual departure. There had been no intention to fly instruments on such a clear night. But it was jump on the gauges or crash into the rocks just north of the runway. It is unknown exactly what kind of gyrations Bill and that T-33 went through, but it was several minutes before Bill was able to look over the edge of the cockpit and thankfully spot automobile lights coming down the Salt Lake City highway into Vegas. Whee! The world was back on it's proper axis. Was this trip really necessary?

By the time Mormon Mesa tacan (the first electronic navigation check point after leaving Nellis) passed under the wing, Bill had settled down and was back in total command. His senses, his equilibrium, and his grasp of the situation had returned, so on with the flight. What were those bright flashes up ahead? Weather hadn't said anything about thunderstorms between Las Vegas and Denver. Then again, the weatherman hadn't said much about anything. He had been on a coffee break and Bill had signed off the weather portion of his clearance himself. As he drew closer to Grand Junction it was obvious that a line of thunderstorms stood directly in his path. Maybe they could be circumvented by going a little South of course? About thirty-seven seconds into that plan, a big bad cumulonimbus grabbed his tiny airplane and showed Bill he really didn't ever want to mess with Mother Nature. It finally spit him out of the top still in one piece, which was a miracle in Bill's mind. That was the good news, the bad news was the line of thunderstorms were still between him and Denver. It took Bill a minute or so to evaluate the situation, actually it was no more than two seconds to arrive at a decision. What 'Stew' in Denver?

After landing back at Nellis, he called Red Dog and said his crew rest would've expired before getting to Denver, so he decided he had better not complete the flight. Red Dog's comment was, "OK Bill, I'll get the real story Monday morning." What a trusting soul to work for. He then tried to contact his 'Stew', but she was already on the town with other people. What a great girl? And he had braved the dark and turbulent night for her(?).

Well, it wasn't a total loss, he was still in time to hit the Strip with 'the gang'. Nothing like having buddies you could count on. Their comment when he showed up at the bar on top of the Desert Inn Hotel, fondly called "Mobile Control," was, "What did you do, oversleep?" Little did they know!

21

"Please Take a Number"

Aircraft flying overhead in formations have always been a crowd pleaser, especially when the number of planes exceeds ten. There seems to be a mystic attraction when airplanes come flying by in close proximity to each other. It's like some magic hand is guiding the entire formation. It is a well known fact that fly-bys always represent some sort of salute or special occasion, either a change of command, retirement ceremony, or top cover for a parade. In the 50's at Nellis, a sixteen shipper could be put together just by mentioning the word. Today, it would take an edict from J.C. before anyone could get eight planes going the same way on the same day. It just appeared that everything was easier then, or maybe it just seemed that way. It also seemed that every base in the earlier days had some sort of fly-by at least once each month. Somebody was always being retired or transferred, which gave them plenty of reason to get a few airplanes in the air, all at the same time.

Nellis, being the Home of the Fighter Pilot, was going to top them all. They were going to have the granddaddy of all fly-by's. The occasion was to honor Colonel Clay Tice, who was leaving the hallowed halls of Fighter Land for a desk job in Washington (Ugh!). They really wanted something fantastic, so the flying operations guru settled on a 200 F-86 Sabrejet fly-by. It would be one of the largest ever seen, especially since it was to be comprised of only one type aircraft. It was planned to fly down the runway from South to North, past the Headquarter's building, where Col. Tice would be the reviewing officer. It would also prove that Nellis could accomplish the tremendous undertaking of having over 200 F-86's in the air simultaneously. There would be a few additional planes airborne just in case a spare or two was needed. That many aircraft in the same airspace at the same time was almost unheard of, even in those days. They wouldn't have put that many birds in the air for the President of the United States of America, but there is no hill too high for the brave and the mighty. We were going to have a 'Really Big Show'.

There were a few complications to overcome. It wasn't an everyday occurrence to put 200 aircraft into the air with a wave of the hand. First, the powers controlling, had to insure that the required number of aircraft were in commission and capable of flying. Then they had to plan on how they would get them all together once they were airborne, so they could arrive over a point on the ground in a safe and logical sequence. What complicated this particular occasion even more was the fact that half of the F-86 aircraft at Nellis were equipped with UHF radios, and the other half with VHF radios, since maintenance was in the middle of transitioning to UHF. This meant there would be no way to communicate between the front and the rear of this tremendous formation. No one seemed worried about this small detail, since there wasn't supposed to be a lot of conversation anyway. As was always briefed by the 'Big Guys', just put the light on the star and only speak up if you see me on fire.

This spectacular event was scheduled to be held on a Saturday morning, another small hiccup since Friday nights were always pretty good party times. It was a better than even possibility that there might just be a few of the troops a wee bit hungover. Not that this would render anyone unable to fly; a little fog behind the eyes never slowed a charger. In fact, there was a gala planned for the good Colonel on the Friday night just before the fly-by, so it was assumed that those details were taken care of.

The bulk of the flying force was made up of lieutenants, like the six of us. Jim and John K., David, Bob, Glenn, and I had been flying school classmates. We lowly lieutenants had not been invited to the 'Big Dogs' party at the Officer's Club, so we pressed on to do our Friday night thing in the Super Party Town of them all, Las Vegas. We were all bachelors living off base, so there wasn't any problem about coming in late or having to answer a bed check. The six of us were living in a four bedroom house not far from the base. It was a wild place, especially when we set our minds to really partying or having a one-of-a-kind extravaganza. That particular evening we, plus four others living near by, hit the "Strip" for our normal Friday night outing, well aware that we had to make the early morning briefing for the fly-by of all times.

We were home well before our normal turn in time—I was in bed by 1:30 AM—since we didn't want to be late for the briefing. We had all arrived home together in a two car caravan, some a little more in the sauce than others. No one considered himself to be really drunk, or that is what we thought, until we started surfacing the next morning. We were staggering around brushing our teeth and shaving when someone realized that

David wasn't anywhere to be seen. We were sure he'd returned with us the previous night. Somebody remembered him being in the car on the ride back, but his bed hadn't been slept in when we checked. After much deduction—(it hurt to think)—we decided the car was his last known location. When we went out to check, there on the floor of the back seat lay David, snoring to the heights. I guess he was just overlooked when we got out of the car and went in to bed.

David, who was usually as sharp as a tack, didn't come around to what could be considered an alert condition when we hauled him off the floor of the backseat. In fact, he was something between a wet noodle and a willow limb blowing in the wind. It was evident he needed lots of help, and in a hurry, if he was going to be a part of the world's greatest fly-by. We rushed him into a very cold shower as step one of the remedy. Next, we started filling him with the blackest of coffee while keeping him on the move. He wanted to fall into the closest chair or bed at every opportunity, and didn't really seem interested in flying on this momentous day. The "K" twins, Jim and John, were doing the best they could with David, although they weren't the soberest of individuals themselves. They were talking in single syllables and kept saying 'Tom' and 'George', which meant 'Bad' and 'Good' respectively. It was something they must have picked up the previous night. Their conversation went something like; "That's George David," when he would drink more coffee and "That's Tom David," when he wanted to fall into a bed or a chair—real brilliant dialogue for that early in the gray light of dawn.

After more than the usual preparation, the six of us were on our way to the base, and the briefing, in what could be considered fair (?) conditions. Glenn, Bob and I were more than capable of flight; Jim and John were slightly above border line; and David was just barely ambulatory. We walked into the large briefing room and went to our respective flight areas. Jim and John said hello to their Operations Officer as they passed his location, adding a few Toms' and Georges', coupled with some snickers and winks. This immediately got them grounded for the day. Their Ops Officer, for some strange reason, thought they had been drinking excessively the night before. How could he? David went straight to his seat and appeared to focus intently on the briefing screen for the fly-by. You could have fired a gun in front of him, and he wouldn't have blinked. I think rigor mortis was setting in. You guessed it, David wasn't challenged; he remained on the schedule. As soon as the briefing was completed, Glenn, Bob and I hustled David away from the scene and continued the coffee and exercise rehabilitation. Jim and John were still discussing their plight with their Ops Officer but weren't making any headway on a reprieve. In fact, they only cemented their status as ground observers.

Start engine, taxi out, and take-off time was here. The Big Show was on the road. The gaggle was airborne and beginning to form up. This was no mean feat. The first flight of aircraft to takeoff had to continue north, almost halfway to Salt Lake City, before starting their turn back to the east. This distance was needed so the last planes getting airborne would have a chance to cut off the lead planes. This allowed them the time and the distance to get together in the desired formation. The entire group went as far east as the Grand Canyon before starting the swing around well south of Las Vegas. In fact, the southern point of the turn was somewhere near Laughlin, Nevada. The formation was intact, things were going as planned, and the World's Greatest Fly-By was cruising along, headed for its rendezvous with Col. Tice.

The airwaves were fairly quiet—only an occasional, "Blue Flight's in" or "Green Flight is closing on the left." It pays to have half of the ships on a different type radio if you want to keep the chatter down. Oh! There was also an occasional 'George' or 'Tom', mostly in a guttural tone, that I assumed to be David. At least the therapy with the coffee and the walking must have paid off, he was remembering the words.

The total flying time was just over one hour. We were on time and looking good. Flights of four were in a diamond formation. Numbers two and three on each side of the lead with number four in the slot forming a small diamond. Then additional flights were on each side of the lead flight with a fourth in the rear to form a larger sixteen ship diamond. There were twelve of these sixteen ship diamonds, one behind the other with the final eight aircraft tucked on to the rear. We made the formation pass in grand splendor, a sight to behold, not even the slightest problem. THEN WE PASSED THE FIELD; everyone began to loosen their formation positions and started to check their instruments. Some cockpits must have looked like Christmas tree lights, all red and amber, because a large number began declaring emergencies for various and sundry reasons. It was very fortunate not to have to land immediately.

The last thing I recall the tower saying was, "Blue 6, you are number 12 in the emergency pattern."

Well, the fabulous six were together again. Jim and John were disappointed that they had missed the Big Show. Glenn, Bob and I were happy to be out of the crowded sky. And David, finally able to put more than a few mumbles together, said, "Boy, I was afraid to look into my cockpit, who would want to be number 13 in the emergency pattern?"

I guess he was either superstitious or just didn't like long lines!

22

"It Doesn't Always Pay to Advertise"

If I had to select a perfect next door neighbor, I would be hard pressed to have one better than Tommy T. I could have beaten my wife in the middle of the street, and still looked like a saint in the eyes of the air base's family housing area we all lived in. Tommy was not bad to his family or wife, he was just consistently unpredictable. If another fighter jock stayed longer at the club than was expected by his wife, then T.T. was there even longer. If someone came home late from a night on the town with the boys, T.T. wouldn't make it home until the next morning. If a neighbor decided to let the lawn go for a couple of days, T.T. would wait until his was a jungle. Tommy was truly one of a kind. He was also an excellent aviator and one of the more respected fighter pilots at Nellis AFB during the early fifties. He was a member of the Nellis AFB Gunnery Team that won the 1956 World Wide Championships, and was one of the Top Guns in the entire tactical air forces. He was tops in the air, but he did have a propensity to get into trouble on the ground.

Early one Sunday morning I received a telephone call from Tommy. He sounded like he had just gotten in from the strip, although I had heard him pull in about three in the morning. He was never known for being quiet. He said, "Could you come over here for a minute, I've got something to show you?" He was outside by the carport, looking at his Buick when I arrived.

The car was a red and white hard-top, two-door Riviera that was a real beauty. Tommy really loved this car, and always kept it in top-notch shape. He kept it washed and polished at all times. Even when other things needed his attention, Tommy would give priority to his car. This morning, however, it didn't look exactly right. The top of the car appeared as if it had been given a finger wave or a permanent. It was definitely not the smooth and polished surface that always seemed to be there. In addition, both fenders and front grill had some alterations that did not come with the original delivery. It had either been attacked by a ball-peen hammer, or it had been in the worst hail storm ever recorded.

Tommy was forlorn, and he appeared to be at the depths of despair. It would have been wise to insure that there were no sharp instruments close at hand. My first comment was, "What in the world did you run into?" He sadly shook his head and said, "I don't remember, but I think I ran into something on the way home early this morning." That was a gross understatement. It was a certainty that he had hit something; it was just a matter of whether it was animal, vegetable or mineral. I said, "Let's get my car and take a look along the road to the base. If we see something we don't like, we will just keep going. There isn't any blood on your car, so you probably didn't maim anyone or they would still be draped across your hood." Tommy seemed to shutter at the words blood, maim, and draped. He was having enough trouble just keeping his coffee from spilling, a large case of the shakes was slowly encompassing his upper torso. Tommy consented to the proposed plan of action although I don't believe he really wanted to know who or what he had encountered. I couldn't blame him; I wasn't so hot on being his tour guide on this mission either. Nevertheless, we headed out to find the unknown.

The traffic at that time of morning was very light, so we could take our time looking for scenes that were not supposed to be unusual or rearranged. (That's rearranged as if altered by using an automobile to provide a push or shove where it wasn't required.) We made one pass all the way to North Las Vegas at a decent speed without seeing anything that would cause a person to think that someone had deviated from the normal path of traffic flow. There weren't any signs of mangled debris or other disturbed roadside appurtenance that would suggest that T.T. had deviated from the traveled way last night. No one we saw along the highway appeared concerned about earlier events. Maybe we should go and ask the police?

It was a known fact, that personnel from Nellis had to be careful when dealing with the North Las Vegas (NLV) Police. It wasn't that they issued tickets only to airmen from the base; it was just very easy for them to recognize a car from the base and pull it over if it was deviating from the norm in the least way. In fact, it hadn't been long ago that one of our troops, by the name of Nogo, had been tagged for his third violation. He had been trying to make it back from an all-night party when he finally decided it would be better to pull over for a short nap rather than get caught for driving under the influence. About dawn, he heard a knock at his window. Standing there was one of North Las Vegas's finest, telling him to wake-up and roll down his window. The policeman, who was familiar with Nogo and his white Lincoln Continental, said, "Driving and drinking again!" Nogo was upset with that remark; he had gone to all the trouble to stop and park so he wouldn't get another ticket. Why was he being accused of such a deed? "No way," cried Nogo, "I just pulled over to get a little sleep before going home." "Then why did you park here?," asked the man in blue. Slowly Nogo eased out of his car and surveyed the immediate area, only to realize he had parked straddling(?), A RAILROAD TRACK! Luckily, it was just a spur and not the main line, but Nogo had to admit that the police had a good case against him. They always leaned pretty heavy on circumstantial evidence.

Anyway, you can see why we certainly didn't want to ask the NLV Police if they knew of any unusual occurrences last night along the base highway. So we started a slower drive back toward the base, this time looking for tire tracks that had departed the proper lane. We had gone only a few miles when we spotted the most unusual Billboard. It had the oddest opening at the very bottom, just the size a car would make if it had driven through. We stopped and went for a closer look. The sign was anchored to the desert by thick round telephone poles, spaced just wide enough for a standard size car to get through. Something had entered from the south side of the sign and departed the north side, without making contact with any of those poles that were capable of stopping a Sherman tank.

Tommy had threaded a needle! The tire tracks were perfect, straight through the center of the sign, curving immediately back up to the road as if it had been designed that way. Needless to say, we didn't linger at the scene. Tommy got his car repaired, the sign had a broken bottom panel for months, and the NLV Police (to our knowledge) never did figure out just who had tried to alter US 93 between North Las Vegas and Nellis. They couldn't even connect Nogo with this one; although I am sure he was a prime suspect.

I think I mentioned earlier about how the Good Lord must look after drunks, fools, and fighter pilots. Last night, He was working overtime.

"The Weather Outside Was Frightful"

We had been to Hamilton Air Force Base (AFB) on one of our quarterly air defense deployments. The secondary mission at Nellis required each flying unit to visit their assigned West Coast base. This enabled the squadron to stay familiar with operating procedures, and to keep their skills honed with the air defense establishment. It was a particularly coveted trip for us since we usually had McClellan as our deployment location. To get a chance at Hamilton was a wonderful opportunity which made it difficult to prioritize the main reasons for being there. The flying was top-notch, it presented a chance to get away from the normal instructing duties, and San Francisco was only a few miles down the road. I am not sure in what priority sequence the above would be aligned, but maybe a combination of flying and the big city, would be a good guess. This particular trip had been outstanding. The weather had been exceptional, the flying was above normal, and the activity in the 'city by the bay', went way over the stupendous mark.

We had finished flying early Saturday afternoon, and weren't scheduled to depart for Nellis until noon the next day. It was off to San Francisco for a final evening on the town. We planned to rendezvous back at the Hamilton base operations at ten o'clock, Sunday morning. We would have a quick briefing to collate the necessary flight information. Then, all twelve F-86 Sabrejets would blast off for Las Vegas, and home. That was the plan, what transpired was slightly different.

The final night on the town turned out to be a real 'wing ding'. The party was much more than anyone had contemplated. We had obtained rooms in the Mark Hopkins on a 'one time' special deal that someone had worked out. It was probably Ray L., who could charm a snake without having to use a flute. It started with a mandatory formation at the Top of the Mark. Five o'clock cocktails for everyone. It lasted for several hours. The management loved us. We were hardly boisterous at all. Finally, just before we were about to be tossed out on our ear, our crowd started to dissipate. Groups of three or four went their merry ways. It was mostly; a sumptuous meal, more drinks, and some gaudy entertainment before getting to bed. I was told that the majority made it to bed before sunrise. But that was hard to believe, because the next morning was so overcast you couldn't tell if the sun was up or not. I know I couldn't!

Amazingly, everyone was present and accounted for when the bus departed for the airfield. It was a nasty day. The weather outside was typical of Northern California during that time of year. The rain was coming down in torrents. It was being driven by swirling winds that even made driving difficult. The bus was constantly being rocked back and forth, which didn't help an already queasy condition shared by many. As we crossed the Golden Gate Bridge we were engulfed in the low hanging clouds. It was a gray day, hard to tell where the water and ground started, and where the clouds stopped. Every now and then the churning white caps on the bay could be seen through a break in the water laden clouds. It was a rough ride out to Hamilton AFB and it was still raining cats and dogs when we arrived. We were happy to get off that bus. The drenching rain felt good on my face, and I am sure that was the case with most of our motley group.

Upon entering the operations area, we were informed that the weather for take-off was questionable at best. It seemed that two Navy fighters had departed earlier for Moffet Naval Air Station, just south of the bay area, and they hadn't, as yet, arrived. They had either crashed shortly after take-off, or they had been caught in the turbulent weather during climb-out. Of course, that information was interesting, but we had a schedule to keep. We pressed on with our departure plans.

Ray L. and I were to be the first two off. Naturally, with Ray being one of the detachment commanders and I his chief operations flunky, it would be unfitting for us not to launch our pink bodies into the murky gray, first. We would take-off in two ship elements at five minute intervals. The entire launch sequence would cover a thirty minute span. All we needed was a slight lull in the weather pattern, and we would be home free. The problem was, there hadn't been, and there weren't any lulls expected for the remainder of the day. Now this type of pessimistic forecast didn't set well with Ray. He strode into the weather office and personally examined the current meteorological charts. Just what he expected to find was unknown to us all. After several minutes, he declared that in exactly one hour, we would have the break we required. The weather officer could only shake his head in wonder—the

92

eleven of us slowly raised our eyes to the sky. The rain was coming down harder now than when we had arrived.

We were at our planes, in preparation for Ray's forecasted weather lull. The end of the runway was barely visible from the ramp. The water spray from the waves in the bay was blowing over the breakwater that protected the South end of the base. In a matter of seconds, I was soaked through to the skin, just getting into the cockpit. The clouds were darkening by the minute, it certainly didn't appear to be improving. Nevertheless, Ray and I were ready to start our engines. Just as we were about to punch the 'go' button, a messenger from operations drove up. He informed us that the field was closed. The weather had gone below minimums for take-off. So much for the 'Ray L. School of Weather Forecasting'. The trip out to the aircraft in that driving rain had completely cleared my head, so it wasn't a complete loss. Back inside, we were all milling around waiting for conditions to lift. Ray was back to basics with the weather officer who now was re-established as the chief weather guru. He seemed to think conditions would improve slightly, in about forty minutes. It wouldn't be a complete clearing, but it would be enough to give us a chance to get the group on it's way to home base. It was either that or back to San Francisco. The problem there was, no one had planned finances for the extra night. We were collectively, dead broke. We didn't have an option; give us the take-off weather and we would be on our way.

Miracle of miracles—the weather guesser's prediction was coming to pass. Suddenly, the sky began to lighten, the breakwater at the end of the runway came into view, and the rain slowed to a drizzle. Visibility was up to two miles, and the ceiling was in the neighborhood of four hundred feet. There was a mad scramble to start engines.

Ray and I were in the number one position for take-off. Weather was holding above minimums with a brisk quartering cross wind from the right. Ray nodded his head for brake release, we were rolling. I was on his right wing so the cross wind wouldn't blow his jet wash into my take-off path. We were approaching nose wheel lift off speed when Ray's nose started to rise just a fraction prematurely. A gust of wind caught his right wing almost tipping him over. For a moment, he was in a very precarious position. He immediately put the nose back on the runway, and continued take-off. This maneuver slowed his airspeed just enough to put me ahead as we broke ground. Several sea gulls flushed from the cover of the breakwater as we blasted out over the bay. For a second, I thought Ray had ingested one down his engine intake, but luckily they had missed. I retarded my power so Ray could retake the lead. It was tricky attempting to stay below the clouds and above the water. As I looked back, Ray was steaming up, and going by me like the wind. Quickly, I was back on with full power, which just enabled me to slide in on his wing as we entered the clouds. Wheee! What else could happen? I shouldn't have asked.

As we climbed out on the departure course, the clouds were thick and turbulent. It wasn't difficult maintaining a good wing position, but it did require some jockeying of the stick and throttle. Finally, about five thousand feet before topping the clouds, things began to smooth out. We were home free, all we had to do was turn on course, and head for home. WATCH OUT! Ray's wing jerked sharply down in my direction, forcing me to kick hard left rudder to avoid a mid-air.

"What's going on lead?" I asked in a strong questioning tone.

"My controls are sticking, something is causing them to stick. You having any trouble?" came his answer.

I had noticed a slight jerkiness during the climb out, but just chalked it up to the turbulence we had experienced at the lower altitudes. "Let's get on top, before we experiment too much further," was my reply. We were just breaking in the clear, and I wanted some maneuvering room before we made any more unusual dips and dives.

After a bit of experimenting, it was obvious that we both had some type of control problem. Ray immediately relayed our problem to the other troops still on the ground or in the climb out. "Keep your controls moving, or they seem to freeze up," was his message. For most ham fisted pilots, that wasn't any problem. But for us smooooth flying dudes, it was a different story. Surrrre, it was! After that weekend, very few, if any could even spell smooth.

It may be hard to believe, but we all made it back to the Nellis ramp without even scratching an aircraft or a pilot. A few did experience some harrowing moments when their controls didn't completely free up until they reached the lower altitudes. It seems some of the heavy rain that pounded our aircraft most of Saturday night and Sunday morning, found its way into the bellcrank housing at the base of the stick. The water partially froze, after climbing above the freezing level causing the controls to bind. It certainly wasn't conducive to long life, particularly if high altitude flying was the mission of the day. This condition really became noticeable, and a problem, as altitude increased and control movement diminished. A fix was later implemented by North American Aviation to preclude the problem. A couple of drilled holes in the housing did the trick. Isn't it marvelous what a little ingenuity can do for safety?

We called it the "CURSE of ALCATRAZ." We had to blame it on something, it certainly couldn't have been our fault! Also, I am happy to announce that it didn't deter anyone from returning to Hamilton AFB, or the beautiful "City by the Bay." A little rain couldn't keep us from our appointed boondoggles. We did, however, always get a certified weather person to check for Bay Area meteorological conditions. We wanted to know if extra money, and an umbrella was going to be needed.

"Godfrey Live"

Arthur Godfrey was the toast of daytime television during the late 50's and was respected for his lively and versatile shows. He put everything before the cameras from acrobats, to zoos, to garden parties, to you name it, and he always made it interesting. On this particular occasion, he was in the San Diego area for an entire week, so all his shows were oriented with a West Coast theme. A main attraction scheduled for the last show of the week was the Air Force's precision flying team, the 'Thunderbirds'. He also wanted to exceed the speed of sound during the same live show. Since the Thunderbirds only utilized single seated F-100 Super Sabre aircraft, it would mean that one of the newer two seated versions of the F-100, the F model, would be required for his supersonic flight. At the time, Nellis AFB only had two F models and only a few pilots that had enough time in them to be instructor qualified. I was one of three and as luck would have it, I drew the short straw. I got the privilege(?) of accompanying the team to North Island Naval Air Station for the show and to be Godfrey's personal pilot for his trip through the sound barrier.

Bill Scott, the narrator for the team, was the point man or coordinator for this spectacular that was to be, certainly one of a kind. The plan was to have the team perform just off Point Loma in San Diego with Godfrey helping with the narration. When they cut to the last commercial, he and Bill would jump into his tiny little helicopter and fly to the naval air station. There he would board the F-100F for a quick take-off and smash through the speed of sound before the precious live air time expired. So much for plans!

Naturally you might expect Authur G. would want a few minutes to get familiar with the cockpit of the Super Sabre? There were little things like which levers could and would blow a person out into the blue if that was your intention or unintention. It also might be nice to know which dial or switch would maintain radio communications with the front seat, just in case some important dialogue was needed. But alas, during the three days we milled around, the wonderful 'Redhead' didn't get by for his insurance lesson. I guess a TV star's time can only be spread so thin, hopefully he would be a quick study. Scotty was confident that Godfrey wouldn't have any trouble getting in the rear cockpit, and he would personally give him a checkout before we streaked into the blue. Great!

Speaking of milling around, this was a hurry up and wait proposition. The only people who did anything constructive were the team leader and the narrator. The rest of us either laid around the pool or read a few good books. It wasn't even permissible to get in a test flight to insure the plane would be ready on the big day. Hanging around with the team guys was nice enough, but it wasn't my idea of show business or anything that resembled the fun of flying.

Well the big show day finally arrived, the morning dawned (I think), because the fog was so thick you couldn't see across the street. Wonderful, this was Friday and there weren't any backup days left to reschedule this epic. I had come all this way to be canceled(?), my thoughts on 'Show Business' weren't spectacular, now I was positive it wasn't one of my preferred activities. Things weren't that simple though, the TV moguls wouldn't cancel until the last minute, so we were left hanging like some starlet about to make her debut. The fog was getting thicker by the minute, we could barely find our way across the street to get breakfast. Get serious, Godfrey would be lucky to find downtown San Diego, much less Point Loma. Well someone up high must have wanted to see an airshow, for with only fifteen minutes to cancellation time, the fog swept out to sea and we were left with the bluest of skies.

Ta da! The show was on! The Thunderbirds were airborne and doing their thing. I was sitting in my idling steed waiting for my passenger to arrive. Now the entire show was only an hour long, when the 'Birds' finished their loops and things, there was only ten minutes remaining. The last commercial was in process and Godfrey and Bill were winging their way from Point Loma to North Island; about three minutes as the crow flies. The Navy tower cleared their helicopter in for landing right beside my super sabre. They were shaving every possible second in order to give us a chance to go "BOOM." Godfrey leaped out in bedroom slippers and the brightest orange flying suit I have ever seen. He scrambled up the ladder and into the back seat, pausing only slightly to give me a quick handshake. I could have been Hogan's goat and he wouldn't have known the difference, but at least he looked like he cared. I must say he had guts, or he was fearless when it came to jumping into airplanes with unknown types.

The time was rapidly ticking down, finally after a few seconds of life saving instructions, Scotty got him tied in tight. Canopy down, full power to get to the end of the runway— Oops!—the camera covering the action on the ramp was blown back a bit when the jet blast hit it. So much for hazardous duty pay for the cameraman. He should have expected a fast getaway. The tower cleared us on and off with no restrictions. All the while I was trying to explain to the 'star of the show' how lucky we would be to get this thing accomplished before the hour glass needed to be turned upside down again. Sam Johnson, the T-Bird solo guy, joined us at the apex of our afterburner climb. As we rolled over and pointed the nose at Point Loma, Sam turned on his smoke so the cameras could pick us up. There was only a second or two remaining, the mach needle approached 1.0, it quivered and hung at .97 as the sound barrier was reached. I pumped the stick to get the mach gauge to indicate our actual speed and just before the live air time concluded, the sonic boom almost knocked the covering cameras off the tip of land called Point Loma. Whee! That was cutting it close.

As we roared back up for altitude, Godfrey wanted to do it again. He was a true aviator and a frustrated fighter pilot for sure. We were having a ball. He was doing a few dips and rolls, just enjoying the feel of a powerful machine that could be maneuvered with the slightest of pressures from your fingertips. He sounded giddy and I began to wonder if his oxygen was connected when he said, "Let's go blow over a few sailboats, or maybe strafe the CBS TV tower." (I think his network was NBC).

Just about then, the Master Caution Light ignited, indicating some malfunction. This immediately caught our attention, so strafing was out. We checked the individual system lights and found one of the hydraulic systems that operated the flight controls had gone south. I diplomatically said we had better land, and he seconded the motion without hesitation. He apparently didn't desire to test that extensive ejection seat briefing Scotty had provided just prior to flight.

We made it back to the parking area without further incident, a solid forty minute flight with speeds and thrills unsurpassed in that day and age. He was very grateful, he said anytime I wanted to ride in his little helicopter (and I emphasize little), to let him know. I was just as gracious when I said he would be the first person I would call when I wanted to cheat death in something that looked like a bubble gum machine without the gum. He just gave his jovial laugh and was off and going before my words were hardly formed.

It was very interesting being close to a true whirling dervish, but I think I will be happier behind those bright lights of 'Show Biz', rather than in front. The cost of dark glasses will be far less, for sure!

"We Also Fly Airplanes Between Games"

The mission of the Fighter Weapons School (FWS) was to train fighter pilot instructors. After students completed the course, they returned to their units with the capability to organize and operate a complete gunnery program. They had the knowledge and expertise to solve most of the situations that arise in the field concerning weapons delivery and fighter deployment. They were, and still are, the best of the best.

The organization that trains these super fighter pilots had to maintain a cadre of top notch instructors as well as the support personnel to insure a smooth running unit. It was a one of a kind squadron in the late 50's; in fact, it was reorganized and reoriented prior to changing commands by our esteemed Commander, Colonel "Buckshot" White. He convinced Tactical Air Command (TAC) of the need for the Fighter Gunnery Squadron to become the USAF Fighter Weapons School, and be incorporated as a part of TAC, instead of remaining in the Air Training Command (ATC). All of this became a reality in 1957. The unit was rebuilt as a completely self sustaining organization with its own supporting units, such as maintenance and avionics. In all, there were approximately 800 people and two squadrons worth of aircraft. It was efficient and concise, and it was smack in the middle of Fighter Land, Nellis AFB, Nevada.

Col. Buckshot was a stickler for getting the mission accomplished, and he was also a great sports enthusiast. He wanted this newly revamped unit to support the Nellis AFB sports program to the maximum extent possible. In fact, he ordered me, the unit Athletic Officer, to win the Base Commander's Trophy. I had heard of a lot of direct orders in my career, but win a base trophy wasn't one of them. Roosevelt told Eisenhower to, "Take the Continent." Lincoln told Grant to, "Win the Peace." Moses told the Red Sea waters to, "Part." But I had never heard anyone say to an up and coming Captain, whose main interest was in flying, "Win the Commander's Trophy"!

Orders were orders, so I set about determining just what kind of problem this would be, and what kind of athletic talent existed in this great and wondrous flying organization. The plan was to compete in every single sporting event that the base sponsored. Just competing would gain a number of points towards the ultimate capture of the trophy. The events included golf, tennis, softball, basketball, swimming, billiards, ping-pong, badminton, horseshoes, and volleyball. There wasn't a sport known to man that was excluded. If it was rolled, thrown, batted, putted, tossed, or had any way to compile a score, it was included. The squadron could win points for entering a team in a sport, for placing in the league, for winning the league, or for winning the tournament. It was our intention to do them all, and not let any event slip by without some type of participation by the checker scarf troops from the Fighter Weapons School. Oh, I forgot to mention that Chess and Checkers were also included. We were in luck, if the playing boards were ever missing, we could use our scarves to play on. I didn't ask if we could get any points for that.

As the period for trophy competition progressed, we were more than holding our own in the major sports. We won our league in softball and played and placed in the league tournament. We won both the basketball and the volleyball leagues, plus the tournaments. We were heads and shoulders ahead of the other units in the major sports competitions. In the minor sports events, we were almost as powerful. We had a par golfer, an expert table tennis player, and an old timer who threw nothing but ringers in horseshoes. We even had a female that had almost been a professional badminton player before she entered the Air Force. We were cruising towards the Trophy with a fair lead over our closest competitor. However, the race wouldn't be over until the end of summer, and that meant that swimming and diving could be a major factor in the final outcome of the Trophy race.

We were in a slight bind when it came to the water sports. We had one bona fide swimmer in the entire squadron. He was like a motor boat when he hit the water. We just had to make sure he was headed in the right direction, and that he didn't bang his head when he reached the end of the pool. Our problem was, there were a lot of points given for the number of contestants that each unit entered, plus points for the place and show finishers. We were limited in depth since our one fish was "It." As to diving, we had one or two individuals who, with luck, could maybe fall head first off the end of a diving board. We were in trouble to say the least.

We barely held our own during the entire swimming competition. Our motor boat swimmer was about all we had.

We did gain a few entry points by using people with water wings, but we had no other winning point makers except our troop with the webbed toes. He won the first two events, but even he had to sit out a race, to keep from getting completely water logged. The diving hadn't gone any better. We got the points for showing up, but other than splashing a lot of water out of the pool on each attempt, we didn't excel. Our guy who did the cannonball for his final dive, didn't even get any points for the dive. I guess the judges weren't waterproof.

The final day of the swimming competition arrived, and the breast stroke event would be the last chance for us to make any points. We needed to sweep the event if we were to clinch the Commander's Trophy. We at least had to make a showing or months of work would go down the drain. A loss, and I could look forward to a less than exceptional endorsement on my efficiency report. My leader, who now had come to be known as the "Sports Czar of Nellis," didn't like losers. We were at the pool, and only my water speedster and I had swimming suits on. It was possible to enter three people in this event, so I was desperate to at least glean the entry points. Looking around, I spied my immediate boss and friend Nellie. He had come over to watch this final quest to secure the needed points. I asked him where his trunks were, and he said, "At home." I said "Go get them," and without a 'Why' he did. Luckily he lived close-by or he would have been too late. He was back in a flash asking how to do the breast stroke. We jumped in the water, and I gave him a quickie 'how to' on the finer points of the breast stroke, of which I certainly wasn't very conversant.

It was time, we were in the water, the race was on. We won!, We swept the top three. Nellie came in SECOND—I came in third. Either he was a natural, or I had missed my calling and should have been a swimming coach!

But most of all, I could get back to my flying and leave sports to others. We had won the Commander's Trophy and Colonel Buckshot was overjoyed, which didn't hurt my feelings or my career. Thank goodness he wasn't there for the next season. Even the Redskins have trouble repeating in the Super Bowl, sometimes!

"Just a Whisper Should Do"

The Training, Research and Development (TR&D) section of the Fighter Weapons School (FWS) during the fifties did most of the air-to-ground and the air-to-air training projects for the F-100 aircraft. Initially, the F-100A was used, but later the A models were exchanged for D models. These were picked up directly from the North American aircraft factory in Palmdale, California. We would usually send a couple of pilots down in a transport plane, and they would bring back two brand new F-100D's. It was a very quick flight from Palmdale to Nellis, so the time expended was relatively short, just a down and backer over lunch time. The new D's were almost a completely different aircraft from the A's. The flying characteristics were about the same for both, the D being a better and more powerful aircraft. It had more thrust in the engine, updated avionics, increased under wing weapon carrying capacity, and wing flaps that gave it better handling characteristics in the landing pattern. However, the instrument and switch arrangements in the cockpit were completely different. On this particular day, a couple of troops, Tommy T. and Jake, went down to Palmdale for their initial pick-up of two new D models. Both were veterans with above average flying time. Tommy, a happy-go-lucky type on the ground, was all business when it came to flying. Jake, an All American linbacker for a midwestern college, could handle fighters just as well as hard charging running backs. He was a rock of a person, one you would certainly want on your side in any street brawl.

They breezed into the factory complex without fanfare and completed the required paperwork necessary to allow the transfer to occur. They were in a rush to return to Nellis, so they didn't stop for lunch or anything. In fact, they said they didn't need the offered cockpit check-out that the factory types always provided to people who might not be totally familiar with the new cockpit arrangement. They filed the necessary flight plan and were out and in the airplanes before anyone could bat an eye. Starting the engines was no problem at all. They were ready to taxi out for take-off, and had called the control tower for taxi instructions. Tommy T. was leading the flight of two. He called for the flight to check in, "Checker flight, check!" "Twoop" was the sharp answer from Jake. Here were two professionals from the TR&D Section of the FWS looking and sounding their part. Tommy pulled out of the parking space first and proceeded towards the end of the runway. Jake was behind and slightly staggered to the right to keep out of the engine exhaust of T.T.'s aircraft. It was one of those hot days in the desert when you could see the heat waves shimmering up from the pavement. Both aircraft were moving along with their canopies open, trying to keep the cooling wind in their face to off-set the high temperatures.

They finally reached the number one position for take-off, and were waiting on the taxiway for their final clearance to depart. Tommy looked over at Jake and tapped the top of his helmet, which was the signal to close the canopies. T.T. followed immediately with a sharp, curt nod of the head and closed his canopy, expecting Jake to do the same. He was ready to call the control tower for clearance to blast off. Jake's canopy hadn't budged, he had inspected every inch of the cockpit, and the canopy switch was no where to be found. He had looked in every nook and cranny, to no avail. He was just about to tear his hair out. Here he was sitting on the big factory airfield with hundreds of hours in the F-100 type aircraft, and he couldn't find the canopy switch. There was no way he could take-off with it open; it being a clam shell type. However he was desperate enough to have given it fleeting consideration. He was frantically waving his arms at Tommy trying to get his attention. Finally Tommy spotted the antics coming from Jake and noticed that his canopy was still open. Again he tapped his helmet and gave the signal to lower canopies. All that he got back from Jake was a shrug of the shoulders. Jake was down to his last straw, he couldn't get his dilemma across to the lead aircraft. He had no other choice. He would have to call Tommy T. on the UHF radio, and ask him where the damn switch was hidden.

Jake screwed up his courage and reluctantly pressed the mike button. He figured he could whisper to Tommy over the radio in hopes that the whole world wouldn't be listening in. (Now there is no such thing as a whisper on UHF radio). Jake's transmission sounded something like this to him, "Tommy, where is the damn canopy switch?" The rest of the world heard it as, "Tommy, where is the damn canopy switch?" Tommy, not expecting to hear his name, spun around and looked at Jake. "What did you say Two?" Tommy blasted back at him. Again

Jake tried, "Where is the canopy switch?" "Sorry Two, say again, I didn't understand you!" About this time the control tower apparently couldn't stand it any longer and said in a very flat and sarcastic tone, "He wants to know where the canopy switch is located!"

As always happens, no sooner had the transmission been made than Jake spotted the canopy switch hidden up under the left canopy rail. He couldn't get it closed fast enough. He felt about three inches tall and only wanted to get out on the runway and off that airpatch. He growled into the mike, "Disregard lead, I finally found the SOB." They weren't certain, but they thought they heard a slight chuckle from some source, but it may have just been their imagination.

The flight of two taxied onto the runway and made one of the smartest formation take-offs ever witnessed. Jake had his wing tucked in as tight as possible and sat like a rock as the two Super Sabres climbed majestically into the air. They would have put the "Thunderbird Acrobatic Team" to shame. One thing could always be said about these troops—maybe they didn't know where all the switches were, but they were certainly 'Flying Sons of a Gun'.

"The Commander is Never Late"

During the '58 Gunnery Meet held at Nellis AFB, the USAF Fighter Weapons School (FWS) instructors were not permitted to participate in the competition. They were ruled ineligible from being members of the Nellis gunnery team, for what reason, it's still not clear to me. Regardless, that is the way it was, and at the time there was no recourse. Either we were too good to participate or we weren't wanted, probably too much talent. HA! That left a bunch of unemployed aviators with not much to do during meet time. It was decided that the FWS instructor pilots (IP's) would become the main bulk of the air show and fire power demonstration to be put on at the Indian Springs gunnery range. That meant a firepower show would be flown each and every day during the meet. It would include all types of weapons deliveries, aerial dart launch and firings, Sidewinder missile firings, and the entire gamut of things that could be done with weapons and fighter aircraft. We were to have both old and new aircraft starting back from World War I days up to the present time. It would be a galaxy of fighter aircraft from the old biplane Spads to the modern jets of today. We even had such famous aviators as Bob Hoover doing his thing in a souped-up F-100 SuperSabre, a show that every fighter pilot would always go out of his way to see. It would be the fire power demonstration to end all demonstrations.

There was no stone unturned in preparing ourselves for this responsible task. Timing was down to the second and everyone knew exactly when and where he had to be from briefing, start engines, taxi, take-off and right on though the entire mission until the Time on Target (TOT) occurred. The entire squadron was a well oiled watch, from the Commander (Buckshot by name), to the most junior Captain in the outfit. However, after several days of the same missions, the same deliveries, the same flight paths, the same old everything, it became quite possible for one to get a little bit complacent. This was particularly true if things had been going along in a very outstanding manner, which they had. There was a gnawing feeling that something or someone would break the exceptional chain that had been established. Naturally, it wasn't to be the most junior Captain that almost caused the entire reputation of this august outfit to go down the drain. You guessed it— Buckshot, our esteemed leader, our guru of checkered scarves, the headmaster of this talented group, was the one that almost put an end to our perfect record of "On Time Deliveries."

As the story goes, we were all standing around in the squadron coffee bar having our morning intake of the black stuff while waiting for our individual times to put on our part of the show. We were drawing to the close of our demo duties and were about to get back into our everyday roles of fighter gunnery instructors. We were ready. This had been fun, but day after day of the same old routine wasn't what we had in mind. If we had wanted to do the same thing all the time, we would have joined the airlines.

No one was paying any attention to the exact time until someone said to Buckshot, "Sir, what time does your missile shot go today?" It was like a bomb had exploded. Buckshot was out the door in a flash, dragging his helmet and parachute behind him. He leaped into the cockpit, cranked the engine, and departed the parking area in a cloud of dust. He hit the runway, lit the afterburner and blasted into the sky like some kind of scalded eagle. In fact, he kept the afterburner on all the way up the valley to Indian Springs, almost creating a sonic boom. He really had a difficult time trying to get his parachute buckled and the cockpit restraining seat belt and shoulder straps snapped just in case he had to make an untimely ejection. He was a whirling dervish in a green flying suit on that particular day.

Well, our on time delivery record for the firepower demonstration of the '58 Gunnery Meet was still intact. Buckshot made good his TOT, the missile was on target and our leader was standing back in the squadron coffee bar approximately seventeen minutes after he had bolted out of the door. He was patiently explaining to us lesser troops just how timing was everything. His flight time for the six previous days had averaged one hour and five minutes. It is always nice to be the leader and never have to explain the total reasons behind your more intricate moves!

"Missiles from Mobile Control"

The mobile control unit at Nellis Air Force Base (AFB) was a necessary evil. It added an extra control element, mainly to insure that each and every aircraft on final approach had it's gear in the down and locked position. It was amazing how many times a few pilots could forget to put those all important wheels in the required configuration. It sure helped on the wear and tear of airplane bottoms. Mobile also served to aid those pilots who might be having a bit of a problem with the pattern or any other discrepancy that caught the fancy of the Instructor Pilot (IP) on duty. Sometimes there was more constructive criticism than was warranted. One disgusted pilot had received so much 'help', he curtly announced just prior to touchdown, "Mobile, when I shake the stick, you've got it!"

The duty was not a desirable one. It put the IP in a position of great responsibility, almost a 'Catch 22'. If everything went according to plan, no one seemed to care what the control officer said or did. If something went awry, he became the number one candidate to hang. Therefore, it was a chore that wasn't on the top of one's volunteer list.

Mobile control units had a long evolution over the years. Early on, they were in fact, mobile. They looked like an observation post on wheels. The large glass enclosed area appeared top heavy setting on four over sized tires. In that configuration, a tug was required for transport. There were a few that were built to fit in the bed of a pick-up truck. These did not require any outside power source, but they did become more expensive because of the dedicated vehicle. When traffic changed landing direction because of a wind shift, the unit was towed, or driven, from one end of the field to the other. This took time, and was tough on the sensitive radio equipment. It also had detrimental consequences on other items that could succumb to a bumpy ride. Finally, some enterprising young jock came up with the idea to put one at each end of the field. This saved time, wear and tear on equipment, and provided for a more efficient operation. The radio equipment had to be duplicated, but that didn't seem to be a major problem to overcome. Just the IP had to change location, which could be accomplished in a matter of seconds. Speed was paramount, particularly when a change in landing direction could cause several aircraft to reach critical fuel states. This was definitely true if two or more flights were about to enter from the previous direction, and had to fly around to a different approach for the new entry for landing. The unit became a necessary entity that was accepted, and expected on most Air Force bases in the fifties.

As mentioned before, the duty wasn't usually one that many IP's volunteered for. However, there were a few that used the opportunity to get some of their ideas, and pet peeves before the Group Headquarter types. One of these was our good and true buddy, Nifty McCrystal. He can be remembered from his fame in Korea and his almost Mig kill. Also, the Security Police at Barksdale AFB will never forget that late night visit and his outer-space helmet(?). Nifty could always be counted on to set a potential problem area straight, or make sure that if one wasn't available, create one.

* * *

One nagging irritant that never seemed to have a permanent solution was the ever extending base leg in the traffic pattern. Inevitably, the position of the base leg would move further and further away from the landing end of the runway. This was especially true when more than one flight of aircraft entered the pattern. This usually caused a long, and low, drag in approach. The mobile control officer was constantly on the air, chiding the offenders to, ... "Bring The Base Leg In .... Come on, Bring It Up To The Field." ..... It was a situation caused by flying just a little further distance over the ground than the guy in front of you. If everyone would turn base leg over the same spot on the ground, the problem could be solved. Well, Nifty had the solution. His Mobile Write-Up Form to Group Headquarters read as follows:

"Recommend that the Headquarters Weenie in charge of better flight patterns purchase a one (1) each; War Surplus Barrage Balloon. The balloon should then be moored to the ground at a point that would be the perfect base leg turning spot for our jet fighters. It should be placed at an altitude so that most pilots could easily see it. (We don't want them running into it.) The balloon should have an attached sign that says in large black letters:

'TURN BASE HERE'. If you want to add, "STUPID," feel free. Signed, Your friendly mobile control officer!"

* * *

It is unknown which headquarters weenie received this vitriolic piece of correspondence, but to my knowledge, there was never a balloon to indicate the proper base leg turning point. I wonder why?

* * *

Nifty was also one of the mainstays for mobile duty during the transition from F-86 Sabrejets to the larger, and more complicated F-100 Super Sabre. The F-100 was not an aircraft that permitted the landing pattern to be flown, power off. It required five hundred more feet of altitude on the initial approach to the overhead break. This produced a pattern that was considerably larger than previous jet fighters. The downwind and base legs were wider, and longer. It demanded that the pilot maintain continuous power until touchdown. The aircraft was also equipped with a drag chute to help slow it to a safe, and smooth stop. In the F-86, the throttle could be pulled to idle on the pitch-out for landing. And the remainder of the pattern could be completed without adding power. The Sabre was the last of the jet fighters that permitted fighter pilots to fly a power-off, overhead 360 degree, minimum time pattern.

Nifty didn't initially agree with the change in patterns between the two aircraft. There must have been an old throw back to his leather helmet, and white scarf days. Nifty was one of the last to accept this power-on approach to landing, when it concerned what was lovingly called, 'A Fighter Plane.' His reluctance was registered in one of his last missiles to the 'Weenies in Group Headquarters'. He didn't single out any one particular pilot, he just grouped them all into the one typical pattern that he detested. It read as follows:

"Aircraft #542 (an F-100) was high on initial approach. His pitchout was very tentative, not crisp and sharp like a normal fighter pilot's. He went so far out on the downwind leg, that he almost went out of sight. (But with my trusty binoculars, I was able to keep him under close observation). His base leg was so far from the field, he was almost closer to Las Vegas than he was to Nellis. I instructed him to bring it up to the field. He immediately added power, and blew dirt for a mile or so before he reached the end of the runway. (It looked like a dust storm coming in from California). After touchdown, he was so disgusted with the entire pattern that he unbuckled his parachute, and tossed it out the back of his aircraft. I really couldn't blame him. I would have probably thrown my helmet with the chute. It is recommended, that if this practice of wide and sloppy patterns are permitted to continue, that Mobile Officers be supplied with extra powerful binoculars. It would also be a time saving device to provide a rubber stamp which says; 'Normal F-100 slipshod pattern.' This would save the officer on duty, countless hours of writing, plus eliminate innumerable derogatory adjectives that describe, a truly lousy landing pattern."

Nifty was transferred shortly after that last mobile stint. The transfer, so it was said, had nothing to do with his advice to those Headquarters Weenies. In fact, if the truth be known, some of those weenies were still looking up the meaning to words like; desecration, mephitic, pestiferous, and the like. Everyone sure hopes that rubber stamp is coming soon.

* * *

There were many other incidents and characters during six years at the world's greatest fighter base, but alas—one couldn't stay in paradise forever. It was off to an overseas fighter unit—time to see what was going on in the rest of the fighter world. Maybe one of these days we could come back to this valley of the sun, this entertainment capital of the world, and this base that produces the best flying this side of any war. But for now—off to the Far East—one more time. I hope my eyes don't slant!

Part Three

PHILIPPINES

When I was assigned to Clark Air Base, on the island of Luzon, in the Philippines, it was the anchor for the bases that stretched the length of the Far East. The early 1960's were the years before the Vietnam conflict. Fighter experience had decreased since the Korean War. Many of the fighter units had switched their emphasis to nuclear deliveries, and had let their conventional skills wane. Very little time or effort was spent on aerial combat training or other conventional type weapons. Therefore, the level of readiness during that time frame slowly ebbed. Some of us did what we could, but when things really got going in South Vietnam, our level of readiness had a long way to go. These stories cover some of the instances and individuals who participated in those pre-Vietnam years. The degree of experience ran the gamut, but it is a relative snapshot of what existed in the fighter world for that period in time. As in the previous sections, these stories reflect some of the humor that has always been a part of fighter flying.

"The Party Suits"

Mike and I were old buddies from as far back as flying school. We had completed combat tours in Korea and had just spent several years instructing at the Fighter Weapons School, the Home of the Fighter Pilot. The instructor force at Nellis AFB was mainly captains, and we were right in the middle of that captain grade structure. It was an odd feeling to find that we were to be the top ranking captains of a Pacific Air Force (PACAF) line unit. Our pending assignment to the 510th Tactical Fighter Squadron (TFS) at Clark Field in the Philippines, would enable us to have an impact on squadron matters and decisions that could affect all flying personnel for the next few years. The 510th TFS was one of two squadrons belonging to the 405th Fighter Wing. It was the tactical squadron, flying F-100's while the 509th, flying F-102's, had an all-weather mission. The 510th was unique, in that the squadron color was purple. Most tactical squadrons had either yellow, blue, or red, but the 510th was certainly different in that aspect.

Mike and I both had been in squadrons that had been impacted by newly arriving ranking officers who opened their mouths before they knew what was really going on. We vowed that we wouldn't be that type. On the flight over, we decided that we would just sit back and listen for the first few days. We wouldn't make any waves that might put us in that 'Know it all' category. We would let the status quo remain before attempting anything that could be construed as trying to change the world.

It was a commendable resolution, but sometimes it is very difficult to listen to people that seemed to want to self-destruct. The first squadron meeting we attended illustrated this fact. The major topic of discussion centered on whether the troops should buy 'Purple Party Suits.' This was before the Vietnam Southeast Asian conflict, and party suits, colorful replicas of the normal flying suit, weren't all that well known, particularly, to a couple of recent 'State-Side' troops that hadn't been in the Far East for the past few years. We had never seen any such animal during our combat days in Korea, and we hadn't had any trouble partying there. While party suits weren't all that expensive, it was still an unnecessary expenditure—the money could be better used for booze.

113

The discussion was going hot and heavy with no clear consensus of whether to acquire, or not to acquire. In fact it was almost split down the middle, although the current operations officer that was conducting the meeting, was pushing hard for purchase. I guess he wanted to leave his mark on the unit, and I must admit purple suits would certainly do that. Finally, in what must have been his last effort to push through the acquisition, he focused his attention on Mike and me—the two new guys. We were sitting quiet and amused on the back row. This was a real power struggle for an individual that was losing his hold on the reins of authority. He drew himself up to his full five foot eight inches, and with hope of acceptance in his voice, said, "Why don't we ask the two new troops what they think?" We were hesitant. Hadn't we said that we wouldn't come in as 'Know it alls'? But this decision was to be a landmark issue. It was going to be something that we would have to live with when this character was long gone. Only seconds after the words were out of his mouth, Mike jumped to his feet. The thought of deferring our comments, as was agreed on, flew out the window. Mike, all six foot one of him, scrutinized the assembled pilots, and voiced these sage words of advice: "Why don't we just use the green ones they give us?" A hush fell over the room! The Ops Officer knew immediately that his purple party suit was a lost cause. Discussion was over, finished. There would be no purple suits for this crowd. In fact, that ended the meeting. So much for trying to keep your mouth shut.

The subject of any type of 'Party Suit' never surfaced again while we were in that squadron. Needless to say, the 510th TFS did all their partying, for the next few years, in the tried and true K-2 green flying suit. After all, this hadn't been the time to play the closed mouth new guy. Mike had come through in true fashion, concise and to the point. We could, and did, drink in anything!

"From an Acorn Grows a Tree"

The early sixties was a time in the Air Force when a lot of people were trying to find their niche in the flying game. There had been a large withdrawal of pilots in the late 50's, from the Tactical Air Command (TAC) to the Strategic Air Command (SAC). This had left many young pilots wondering what would happen to them if they attempted to stay in fighters. Would they have a chance to make a career doing what they really wanted or would another purge alter their chosen course just when they were getting good at real flying? This was the attitude of some of the new fighter pilots that reported to Clark Field in the Philippines to join the 510th Tactical Fighter Squadron, in the 1960-61 time frame. Everyone of them was eager to be the best there was, and each worked very hard at doing their utmost to insure that they would stay in the 'Fighter Game' for as long as they desired. Now this made for ideal situations for the squadron flight leaders and the operations officer. Every individual seemed to be ready when called and was more than willing to learn more about their chosen profession.

The aircraft assigned to the 510th was the F-100 Super Sabre, which was a solid bird. A pilot had to take charge of it or it could take charge of him. These new troops had completed a combat crew training course prior to reporting to the squadron, so their aircraft handling capabilities weren't a major problem. They could take-off and land and do the basic weapons deliveries, but they weren't totally skilled in all the various weapons deliveries that our combat mission required. They also hadn't fully qualified in all the air-to-air refueling modes, which was a key part of our day and night requirements. But as I said, they were eager, and they were dedicated to the mission we had to accomplish.

One particular individual still stands out when I think back over those fun days in the early sixties. It had to do with night refueling, which wasn't always the easiest mission to accomplish. This was particularly true when fueling from a KB-50 tanker on a dark, dark night in very rough air. The KB-50 was a converted bomber that could reel out three fueling hoses. One trailed back from the tail end of the aircraft, and one extended from each of the wingtips. Each hose had a circular basket attached that allowed the refueling booms on the fighters to receive fuel when they were coupled together. It also must be remembered that the hose was very flexible, and it wasn't the easiest of tasks to put the refueling boom of the fighter into the trailing hose from the tanker. It was akin to pushing a wet noodle up a telephone pole with both hands tied behind the back—fun to try, but difficult to accomplish on the first attempt.

The KB-50's were stationed in Japan and rotated down to our base every three months. This made it extremely important that we scheduled and received all of our air-to-air refueling requirements, both day and night, while the tankers were available. It was a chore, but not overly difficult to accomplish if each jock made each refueling sortie count. The only critical times were the night sorties, which were at a minimum. If turbulent air was prevalent in the refueling area, pilots didn't have an over abundance of tanker time to share if someone ran into any difficulty. Such was the case on this particular night.

As the Operations Officer, I was scheduled to lead a night refueling flight. One of the newer jocks, I will call Chuck, was slated to fly as the number four man on the mission. He was a natural pilot and certainly one of the more eager of the new arrivals. He was out to make sure he would stay in the fighter force of the Air Force for the rest of his career. He did nothing but think 'fighters' and wanted to be the best in any and every thing he attempted. There is nothing wrong with that attitude, in my mind. If a pilot didn't think he could be the best, there is no way he would be. It does have to be tempered a little bit from time to time, or he could get so intense that he would defeat the goals that he had set out to achieve. This wasn't Chuck's problem—he just didn't want to have the least flaw associated with his flying record.

The mission proceeded as briefed and every phase was going very smoothly. We had briefed for the flight to go in order on the tanker. I would be first, then two, three and four. If we had enough time, we would re-cycle through to get the practice. Night refueling was always a challenge regardless how many times a pilot attempted it. So when number four had attempted several stabs at making contact with this elusive refueling hose, he naturally began to tense up just a little bit.

"Black Four, what's your fuel state?" I was asking him how much gas he had remaining. If he couldn't take fuel from the tanker, he was going to have to return to base without completing his refueling requirements, and without attaining the other mission outlines. "I'm OK, Black Lead. I've got plenty of fuel. No sweat sir, I'm fine." With that retort, I knew he was beginning to run close to the Bingo (minimum fuel for return to base) we had set for the mission. "OK, Four, move out and relax, re-trim and you can give it another try after Black Two gets off the left side."

At this point I knew he was uptight and wanted dearly to complete a hook-up and finish the mission as expected. It wasn't totally his fault. Here he was on his first night refueling attempt, in some of the toughest conditions ever. Even the Element Leader (Big Mike) and myself had both been hard pressed to get on and complete our fuel transfer. It was some of the most turbulent conditions that I had ever encountered. Here we were, expecting a brand new Second Lieutenant to ease in on his first try out of the box. The hose and basket were moving up and down like a child's yo-yo on a long string. Contact was truly a hit or miss proposition. It was like trying to nail Jell-O to a moving wall from a rocking row boat, if that gives you any frame of reference to the degree of difficulty.

"Black Four, what is your fuel count?" I wanted to know exactly how much gas he had, not just an 'OK,' for at 800 pounds he would have to head back to the base and land. We were cutting it as close as possible. "Black Four with Bingo plus two," was the clipped answer. "Alright Four, Two is off, move into position and get your off-load." I was really pushing hard on this top-notch troop. He was what a commander wanted as a new breed. He did not lack for guts. In he moved, tanker bouncing and F-100 bouncing, but unfortunately not together. It was like a first class fencing match, with neither contestant able to gain an advantage over the other.

Now the F-100 burns about 5000 pounds of fuel an hour when a pilot is jockeying the throttle on a refueling mission at the altitude we were operating. That meant Chuck only had a couple of attempts remaining before he would have to abort the mission and return to base. He and I both knew we were cutting it closer than desired, but I wanted him to have one more stab. I said, "For Ch---- sake, relax, just caress the stick, don't choke it to death, just hold it as tenderly as possible. Now get a sight picture and make your hook up." His aircraft seemed to bobble for a moment, then it steadied in the pre-hookup position. Slowly, you could see it inch forward, closing on the critical position just before boom and basket contact. This was the point that the less experienced pilots tried to sneak a peek at the boom tip and the basket. For most, this caused a flinch, similar to the look-up on a golf swing. But Chuck didn't make this mistake twice. The refueling basket and the boom were moving up and down on the same frequency. He made solid contact and was in a perfect refueling position. Most importantly though, he was taking on fuel.

I could almost see the broad smile behind the oxygen mask. It seemed like the pitch black darkness of that F-100 Super Sabre cockpit was just a little bit brighter. Another well qualified fighter jock was doing what he loved best! It's never easy, but if things were too easy, then there really wouldn't be any satisfaction in an accomplishment. The challenge and the skill which it takes to master it, makes the doing worthwhile.

It might be coincidental, but it seems I heard of a Chuck, something or other, that later made quite a name for himself as a fighter pilot. I think his name was Boyd or something like that. Seems he had an outstanding record during the Southeast Asian conflict, and if memory serves me correctly, this fighter pilot ended up with four stars on his shoulders—not really unusual for a Second Lieutenant fighter pilot. One that knew he had what really counted, particularly on a dark night in the skies over the Philippines.

31

"Never Forget the Time"

The F-100 aircraft during its lifetime had to undergo several modifications, either to the engine or some part of the airframe. One of the more noticeable changes to the pilots was the one made to the size of the cockpit instruments. In fact, the entire arrangement of the instruments on the front panel was changed. They had to make room for a few more gauges and dials, so the normal large instrument face size was changed to very small. Adequate to see, but a pilot had to know exactly where to look. Cockpit orientation was taking just a bit longer these days because there were a few unexpected relocations.

For the F-100's based at Clark Air Base, this modification was accomplished at Tainan, Formosa. It was also the same place that the 510th Tactical Fighter Squadron based its four ship nuclear alert force. There was always a contingent of pilots that were on site, and ready to pick up a re-modified airplane when one needed to be ferried back to Clark. Such was the case when I asked "Pie" Ellis to bring a just released F-100 back from Tainan to Clark. Pie was a veteran fighter pilot with over 1000 hours in the F-100 type aircraft, which for that time frame was more than the average jock. He had a good touch when he flew and was considered one of the better pilots in the squadron. But on this particular day, Pie might have been at just a little less than his usual sharpness. Maybe it was because of the previous night on the town, or it was too early in the morning, or whatever normal excuse that could come to a person's mind when faced with an unusual occurrence. Anyway, that is a little ahead of my story.

Pie made the flight back to Clark without serious incident and was happy with a chance to get back a little earlier than normal from his alert tour. He came into the operations office as usual, and in the course of the conversation, I asked him, "How was your flight?" He stated, "Just fine," and then he sort of paused and took a deep breath before he told me the following: "Well I must admit, it was a little different. I started the engine and really didn't pay a lot of attention to the cockpit layout, everything seemed about normal, and it was early in the morning," Pie was very deliberate with his detail. "Tainan tower gave me the usual taxi instructions and clearance for the flight home. 'Plie read, you're creared to Crark by Red 16. Crimb to 25,000 feet and report on course'. They haven't improved any on their L's, but by now I'm use to the ranguage." He pulled his eyelids in a slant to give me the full effect. "I was surprised at the quick go ahead from the Tower since they usually kept a plane waiting for a few minutes just to make sure it had the clearance copied correctly. But this time it was get your ass in gear and get off this airpatch (of course, said in the continued broken Chinese-Amerlican). Well, I immediately obeyed and rolled onto the runway. I engaged the afterburner and was going like a scalded dog in a matter of seconds. As I started to approach nose wheel lift-off speed, I glanced down to check my airspeed and Whoa Ho! It wasn't there. In fact, I didn't see anything that was immediately recognizable. Where in the H___! had all the gauges gone? As my airspeed increased, my scanning of the instrument panel went from fast to faster, and my vision became less and less focused. The only thing I was seeing was the blank spaces between the gauges." Pie moved his head back and forth to add emphasis to his dilemma. "By this time my airspeed was building past what I felt was normal for takeoff. I was falling into a deep quandary, I couldn't find the d___ airspeed indicator. So, I just pulled back on the stick and the bird leaped into the air. At this point I finally focused on the instrument panel and the only thing I could recognize was the clock. I can officially say that I took off at exactly 7:17 AM, Formosan time."

Pie wasn't at all concerned about the incident. He just marked it down to that long list called "Experience"! I, on the other hand, was pleased to know that Pie had come away with a bit of knowledge that he hopefully would carry forward. When things get bad and you can't determine anything else, it's at least nice to know what time it is!

32

"A Spy in Our Midst?"

We didn't always get visiting flights from the other Far East wings during the week. Mainly the weekends were when the troops would come in from Kadena, Okinawa and/or Itazuke, Japan. We would also send our people up their way on weekend cross-countries. The mission was to get flying time and theater experience by visiting the other locations. However, today was unusual when we got a call from the Operations Officer at Kadena, asking us to give a couple of F-100's a quick-turn. They were coming down to get a strange field check-out and needed to get back before dark. He also added that our old and dear friend "Fire Can Dan" was going to be in the front seat of the F-100F. He was leading the flight of two, and was one of the more renowned pilots in the fighter world at that time. His fame was not only for his flying skills, but for his larger than usual sense of humor, which at times tended to be on the morbid side. He had been the source of several of the better known escapades and practical jokes, both here in the Far East and in the States. In fact, on a previous cross-country flight to Kadena, one of our jocks had found a dead goat in his cockpit when he went out to pre-flight before returning to Clark. It was never proven to be the handy work of Fire Can, but the smart money made him the odds-on favorite. He had particularly taken a liking to a brand new Second Lieutenant by the name of Weeks, who was assigned with us in the 405th Wing. Dan had made him the brunt of a couple of jokes on a recent trip when we passed through Kadena. This seemed to be an ideal time to help even the scales plus try for a little upmanship on Dear Old Fire Lad.

We checked with the Air Police (AP's) and asked if they would like to participate in an unknown aircraft arrival exercise. They were delighted for the opportunity, they must have been ex-SAC air policemen who were used to pointing guns at airplanes. The exercise involved meeting the plane in question with mounted machine guns and other heavy weapons. This would insure that the aircraft and their crews followed instructions. There would be no chance for the unknowns to deviate in any way until they were properly cleared or vouched for by a proper authority. In this case the proper authority was to be none other than 2nd Lt. Weeks. His "OK" would terminate the extemporary exercise. The stage was set, the aircraft were on final, and Fire Can Dan was in for what we hoped was one of his more eventful visits to Clark Air Base.

The Air Police convoyed the two Kadena birds into the aircraft parking area. They had one vehicle in front, one behind, and two covering each side. Their mounted twin 50 caliber machine guns were trained in a deadly manner on the front cockpit that contained a very baffled and confused Fire Can. This was serious business, and they were playing it to the hilt. As soon as the engine had been shut down, they ordered him out of the cockpit. They made him produce his ID and proceeded to frisk him in a not too gentle manner. They had him, hands against the side of the fuselage with feet spread wide. Then they called me forward and asked if I could vouch for the man. I said, with as straight a face as possible, "I have never seen this individual before in my life," and walked quickly away before my laughter became audible. As I moved past the wing, I heard Fire Can say in a pleading voice, "You do too know me!" but I must say that he didn't move an inch.

They then spread eagled him on what was now a fairly warm piece of tarmack. Fire Can was almost beside himself. It was evident that the scales were in our favor, and we had milked the situation to the max. Of course, our next trip to Kadena was going to be another issue, but we had to take advantage of each opportunity when it was available. Lt. Weeks stepped forward and stared down at the prone figure. The pleading eyes were enough to make you shed a tear for our forlorn friend. Finally Weeks said, "I will vouch for Capt. Fire Can Dan."

The exercise was terminated. The AP's were happy. Dan was still confused and busily dusting himself off. He wanted to know what the h___ was going on. A little later at lunch while the Kadena aircraft were being refueled, Fire Can was heard to say, "You guys didn't have me worried at all. I knew you were just kidding, but I wasn't sure if those guys on the twin 50's knew you were kidding!"

Luckily, for Dan, they did!

"It's Tough Blindfolded"

The weather business, at best, is certainly not an exacting science. When commanders are dealing with very volatile, and often varying conditions, the chances at perfection are limited—to say the least. Such was the case, when the 13th Air Force Commander decided he wanted to take his monthly ride in one of the 510th Tactical Fighter Squadron's F-100 Super Sabre jets.

The General commanded all the air force personnel and equipment in the area encompassing the Philippine Islands. He was an old timer, who had been in the old Air Corps when it was in it's infancy. As a matter of fact, he was one of our earliest aviators and had flown some of the first Air Corps' planes. However, he was well aware of what the modern Air Force was doing, and thus the reason for his frequent flights in tactical fighter aircraft. He wanted to do and see it all, and he was admired for his forthright manner. There were too many cases when some commanders didn't know what was going on, and in a few isolated instances, didn't care. Prior to commanding the 13th Air Force, the General had been in charge of the U.S. Air Force Weather Service. That position gave him the global responsibility for providing accurate, and up-to-date, weather information to every Air Force installation in the world—a very difficult responsibility.

On the scheduled day, the General had arrived at the squadron in ample time for the flight. We had briefed, and gotten the necessary flight gear fitted and adjusted. It looked like a routine sortie, but with one slight problem. The weather was tending to be a bit testy. As a matter of fact, thunderstorms were the norm for this day, instead of the usual blue sky of balmy Clark Air Base, in the Philippines. It was raining in all quadrants, not just small sprinkles, we were having heavy, heavy showers. It was a day that a person had just as soon stay indoors, and let the ducks be alone in their element. We offered the General just that option, but he had come to fly, and that is what he intended to do.

There were breaks in the rain, and during one of these, we got out to the aircraft. In fact, for a few moments it looked like the clouds were going to abate, and that we were going to have a nice day for flying. The General was optimistic, maybe he was using his weathered eye to assess the swirling winds and clouds. Immediately ahead of us, two aircraft from the squadron had started their engines, and were taxing out for take-off. We cranked our engine, and were only a few hundred yards behind them. It looked like we were in for a pleasant flight after all. Wishful thinking. Our backs had been to the departure end of the runway during start engine. As we turned out of the parking area, and looked over our shoulder, we spotted the granddaddy of all thunderstorms. It was bearing down on the departure end of runway, and appeared to be headed directly at what would be our take-off point. Now, I had mentioned some heavy rainstorms being in the area, this was entirely something different. It looked like a giant black funnel that could eat jet airplanes for lunch. It was something that I didn't want to launch my pink body into, and I didn't want anyone else to give it a try, just to see what might happen.

Well, I was the Operations Officer, I had better do some operating. I told the General of my concerns. He acknowledged with, "Roger, do what you have to." I called the two squadron birds that were in front of us, which by this time were rapidly approaching take-off position, and told them to hold prior to taking the runway. At least until we could see what the weather was going to do. They heaved a sigh of relief, they didn't want to test their thunderstorm flying skills at this point either. I told the control tower that I would be checking with weather, and immediately switched our radio over to the local weather station channel. I asked for the forecaster. He was on the channel in a flash. "WHAT IS THAT THUNDERSTORM JUST SOUTH OF THE FIELD GOING TO DO?" I blasted out at him before he had a chance to say a word.

During this sequence of events, I hadn't remembered that the General had been the Father of the modern day Weather Service. I had just put the local weather guesser in a tight spot without really meaning too. It was completely unintentional. I was only interested in saving a couple of our troops a rough rough ride at the least—much less the strong possibility of them being spit out the other side of that monster—without their airplanes in tact. So I was all ears, waiting to hear what our esteemed weather phenomenon had to say!

"WHAT THUNDERSTORM?" was the shocking answer.

I didn't even hear the groan from the back seat, I was so intent on changing over to the Approach Control frequency.

Approach Control, which usually handled weather departures and landings, had a Radar capability that could not only track airplanes, but could also monitor and track heavy weather. The weather station had been a bust, so I had nothing to lose with trying these guys. Just in the hope that, they might be watching this monster at the south end of the field.

"APPROACH, what is that T-Storm south of the field going to do?" A crisp voice came right back with, "It's going to come right down the middle of the runway and it's MEAN!" "Thanks a bunch," I said, and was back to the take-off frequency in an instant.

"Hey guys, forget about flying, that monsoon is about ready to hit the area. Take'm back to the parking ramp, and lets see what happens from the ground!" My call to the two F-100's in front of us was greeted with, "ROGERS." Those troops were no dummies.

In the process of switching channels, and talking to all parties concerned, I had been attempting to keep the General up to date on my fears. I also wanted him to know what my ultimate intentions were. I had hoped he was following my trend of logic, but I wasn't sure. He didn't offer any suggestions, or try to influence my decision in anyway. It was like having a mute in the rear cockpit. A pretty high ranking one, if I might say so. One that could cancel my contract if, and when, this episode was over. If he decided that my actions were less than responsible, I am sure the 510th Fighter Squadron would have a new Operations Officer before nightfall. "General, I think we'll take it back to the ramp, and see what happens." "Alright," was his soft, and short response.

We began our long taxi back to our parking area with still no rain, just that ominous black cloud hanging just off the departure end of the runway. In fact, we made it back to the chocks, had shut down the engine, and were getting ready to depart the aircraft when the deluge hit. We quickly closed the canopy, and sat through about fifteen minutes of the hardest rain I have ever witnessed. When it had abated, we were finally able to make our way back to the operations building.

The General wasn't pleased that he had to abort his flight, but said, "We will try it again next week. That was an excellent decision you made. I didn't want to test my 'Thunderstorm' penetration techniques either!"

He then seemed to ponder his next thought for a moment, and said "One of these days, I am going to have to get those Forecaster guys a WINDOW in that weather office."

"The General's Car"

The Commanding General of 13th Air Force had a very eligible daughter and the 509th and the 510th Fighter Squadrons had a whole cadre of young, virile, and single males. These manly specimens were literally trapped on the island of Luzon in the Philippines. There just weren't many nice, pretty, young and available ladies who were even in the vicinity of Clark Air Base. The total number must have been under six. That combination meant that 'Miss Maggie' did not want for companionship. In fact, if there was a need to find one of our bright stalwarts, a call to the general's residence would summon anyone of twenty. The same was probably true for the Ops Officer of the 509th when he was trying to round up a few of his young charges. They were always there when she was home, and they had free time away from the flight line.

For several months, the social energy in and around the upper echelon living quarters was a bee hive of activity. No individual bachelor seemed to have the inside track, it seemed to be an open field—but without fanfare, the possible suitors had been pared down to one. It was very subtle!

As you may recall, the General usually flew with our squadron every month or so. This time the flight scheduling call came in and he wanted Lieutenant Demchuk to be his pilot. Never before had we scheduled the Commander of 13th Air Force to fly with a lieutenant—but if that is what the 'Head Man' wanted, who were we to stand in his way. Serge was one of our outstanding jocks and deserved emerging as the 'pick of the litter'. He was better than the average, well rounded in all weapons deliveries and very smooth in his handling of the F-100 Super Sabre. To say that Serge was nervous would be an understatement. If we had scheduled him on a suicide mission, he would have been more at ease.

The mission went fine. The General was very complementary concerning the aviation prowess of our young jet pilot. What better way to check on a prospective member of the family, let's see if the sucker can fly! It appeared that he had the stamp of approval from the very top. (Mrs. General had liked him from the start!)

Serge beamed when you spoke of his impending nuptials. Even the little brother Tommy liked his brother-in-law to be, what else could be asked of this perfect combination. The date for the wedding was still several months away, so it was business as usual for Serge. Flying when scheduled, performing his share of the alert duty in Formosa, and spending the rest of the time with Maggie. He became an integral part of the household, even the General was speaking to him on a regular basis.

New car deals from the Philippines were very good if the contract/purchase order was made from one of the many outlets that operated at the Base Exchange. Even generals knew that and that is what prompted the 13th Air Force Commander to order his dream car. It was the deluxe version of the classic 'MG', open cockpit and all. It was to be canary yellow, with extra chrome to off set the stylish lines of the low sporty profile. There would be only one like it on Clark Air Base, everyone would recognize 'The Boss'.

As luck would have it, the General had just departed for the States on two weeks of Temporary Duty (TDY), when the car arrived. It looked beautiful sitting out in front of Quarters #1. The temptation to give it a spin was almost overwhelming: It could be defective—maybe it doesn't hit on all cylinders— maybe we'd better check it out so the general won't be upset when he drives it for the first time. All these thoughts were going through Maggie's and Tommy's minds. Let's get Serge to drive and we can give it a test spin. (Capital idea!) Wonder why Serge was a little reluctant to accept this brilliant chain of thought? But his fears vanished when Mrs. General agreed 'It Was The Thing To Do'.

They were off! It was a perfect day for zipping around the base in one of the classics of the auto world. The wind whipping through their hair, the warmth of the sun on their faces, and the love of Serge's life next to him. Well almost next to him, the little brother was wedged in between, urging for more speed. "Let's see what she will do," was his cry as he bounced up and down on the tiny armrest between the two bucket seats. Suddenly the wailing of a siren seemed to be growing in their ears. Sure enough, one of the Air Police's (AP) finest was bearing down on the little yellow car. Serge pulled over to the side and waited for the approaching AP. Oh shucks! How could this be happening to me?

"Could I see your license and car registration, please," were the AP's first words. Gulp!—Another Gulp!—Then from

Serge's mouth blurted, "Officer, this isn't my car, it belongs to the 13th Air Force Commander—Ah, ah— I or we were just giving it a spin, I mean a test drive." "Surrrrre you were," came the condescending voice of the AP. "The general always gets a lieutenant to make sure his car performs properly." Desperately, Maggie was digging for her identification to proved that she was really the general's daughter. Tommy piped in with, "I want to see a lawyer before I say anything." He was really a big help. Now the AP had some doubt, "Let me check with headquarters," and was back at his patrol car to call in for information. Tommy was really with the situation now, "Are we going to jail? Will they put us in handcuffs? Who's going to tell my Dad?" With that last comment, Serge almost fainted.

The AP returned and acknowledged that the car, did in fact, belong to the Commander of 13th Air Force. Although, there was no way he was going to buy the test drive theory. He then presented them with a traffic ticket for driving 39 MPH in a 35 MPH zone. He said, "If you are going to drive the General's car, then I suggest you adhere to the General's rules." He was off with a wave and a smile!

The question of informing the general upon his return that his brand new car had been involved in a traffic violation, was truly excruciating. Serge could see his happy future going up in smoke, maybe his entire Air Force career. This wasn't going to be the easiest of tasks. Maggie wasn't about to take the blame; she said, "Serge was driving" Tommy said, "He had been at the swimming pool" and Mrs. General said, "What car?" Serge knew the General would see the police report as soon as he returned to his office, so the confession had to be immediate.

Serge wasn't a slacker, he had the fortitude and grit that the great men before him had exhibited in cases of extreme stress. He approached the General at the first opportunity and said, "Sir, we drove your car around the block to make sure everything was working properly." "Oh?," came the general's answer. "Yes sir, and I think you'd better get that speedometer checked." "Hmm, does that have anything to do with the traffic violation I have on my desk?" said the general with a slight tilt to his head. "Possibly sir, either the entire Air Police fleet of patrol cars have speedometer errors, or your gauge could be at least three or four miles per hour in error. I think you'll agree it was lucky we checked it out for you."

The general said, "Serge, if you have that much imagination, you've got to get along well in this man's air force!"

--The wedding went off as planned!

"Did Anyone See the Caution Flag?"

Tainan is the typical Formosan city. It is nestled on the plains that are overlooked by the majestic mountains that range the length of the island. Rice fields are the prominent landscape feature, and except for the airbase and the town, appear to be the sole source of agriculture and commerce. The airbase is one of the major Nationalist Chinese installations that dot the western coast, looking towards the menacing guns on the Communist Chinese mainland. We, the United States Air Force, utilized a small portion of their base as our tactical nuclear alert facility. We maintained four F-100D's on permanent alert, and rotated pilots weekly from Clark Air Base, our home field. Six pilots formed the weekly alert force, four on status and two off each day. This permitted each pilot to have two free nights on the town.

Normally these nights on the town consisted of a good meal, some shopping in the local stores, and a quiet evening away from the clamor of the airfield. Occasionally, an impromptu party would spring up when least expected. That meant, more than the one or two drinks before leaving the base, snacks instead of that good meal, and one of those hair raising pedicab races to our downtown quarters. Those occasions only occurred once in a blue moon. It just so happened that on this evening, there must have been a blue moon. There was an extra pilot in town, there to pick up an F-100 from the Air America maintenance overhaul facility. He had nothing in particular planned for his evening, so he fit in very nicely with the two of us that were having our usual single Martini at the small, but adequate officer's club. With three instead of the normal two, this evening was destined to be the granddaddy of all impromptus.

Martinis should only be consumed in groups of two, spaced several days apart. We were on our fourth with only about sixty minutes being the overall elapsed time. The good meal had been replaced by several orders of spring rolls, those little fried goodies with shrimp or something as filling. They did absorb some of the toonie juice, but not enough to bring a normal mind back into any similarity that bordered rational thought. We were on the outer edge, ready for blast off.

Immediately outside the officer's club were pedicabs ready to transport the downtown trade to downtown. Pedicabs are three wheel machines with a bicycle front, and a dual wheel seat cab behind. The drivers were wrinkled old Formosans. They earned their livelihoods pedaling non-walkers from place to place. The pedicab is not an easy vehicle to maneuver and direct. Many may remember the easy time they had as tots with their tricycles. But, when the seat level is raised and the rear end is extended to contain seating for two, it becomes an unruly vehicle only faintly resembling a tricycle. The contraption feels like it could tip over during any attempt to turn, and sometimes does. Increase the speed, and the problem multiples ten fold. It would take a lot of practice to master it's control. If a race for glory is the initial attempt aboard this monster. Hang on!

The first phase of our impromptu party was at an end. We had consumed enough alcohol to keep forty drunken sailors well oiled during an entire shore leave. We slowly sauntered out of the on-base officer's club, smug in our multiple martini glow. We were in perfect control! We were looking for some swift transportation to the downtown area, to complete this wonderful evening. Like a bolt out of the blue, we spied three sturdy pedicabs with their drivers in the ready position for departure. We would each occupy a machine. We discussed betting on whose chariot would arrive at our destination first. Then, as fighter pilots are prone to do, decided that it would be best if we replaced the drivers and controlled our own destiny. It was a great idea, but not to the driver/owners. They weren't about to let three steely (glassy) eyed individuals, in green flying suits, take over the controls of their sole source of income. As far as they were concerned, we could foot race downtown.

The negotiations would have made any first rate diplomat proud. It was a little difficult at first, the language barrier being somewhat of a stumbling block. After much hand waving, and pointing from passenger to driver's seat, we finally went right to the bottom line. A crisp twenty dollar bill put each driver in the passenger seat. There was still a bit of reluctance, but we were mounted at the controls, ready to head out for the three mile dash to downtown Tainan.

Gentlemen, Start Your Pedals!

There wasn't a green flag to be seen, so it was off in a cloud of dust. We were three abreast, striving for a lead position before reaching the first downhill grade. The downhill feature made the initial pedaling easier, but we faced a long

131

gradual left turn, gentle yet demanding. Any turning motion increased the difficulty of operation. Also, the roadways were all dome shaped, with sloping sides to enable rain water to drain into a two foot deep culvert that bordered on each side. This made it very difficult to control the pedicab on any intended straight line course. It always felt to me, like I was being slowly sucked off into that beckoning culvert, or that this monster of a machine was ready to flip me off at any moment. But, in the heat of the race, I didn't let my concentration waver from the task at hand.

We had completed the first mile and were still bunched in close proximity to each other. It was a nice evening with many strollers enjoying the last rays of the Fall season. The street was shaded from the quickly disappearing sun by tall, stately trees which bordered the western side of the street. I wish I could have enjoyed the scenery, but the exertion from constant pedaling (there were no coasters on these machines) was beginning to narrow my field of vision.

The roadway gradient changed from downhill to uphill, and there was immediate pain in my calves and thighs. But, what was a little discomfort, we were in a race that would require the last place guy to buy the drinks. To finish in the top two, was a must!

The pedestrian traffic began to increase as we approached the top of the grade. More people were crossing from one side to the other, so we had to increase our attention to the road, to keep from clipping one of them. Each machine had a bell on the handlebars, so there were many ring-a-lings piercing the evening air. Also, the owners were somewhat white-knuckled in the back. An occasional scream or two was not unusual, and helped to alert the unobservant jaywalker just before he was to become road kill.

We were on the downhill and final stretch. I was leading and could almost taste a cool libation, when suddenly, a family of four appeared on what would be a catastrophic collision course. I had to make an instantaneous decision. I felt that I could miss the mother and father with some distinguished steering, but the two little kids would have been dead meat. In the interest of our diplomatic relations with the Nationalist Chinese, I altered my course to intersect with the concrete drainage ditch to my right. Just as I neared the father, my life flashed before me. I missed him and his family with inches to spare. The pedicab went into a slight skid when it rolled onto the grassy space between the roadway and the ditch. I straightened the front wheel, and eyed the slight lip on the ditch's edge...... Maybe I could jump the ditch?......... Maybe my mother could become an astronaut?...... The front wheel dropped squarely into the ditch, with a resounding thud. The pedicab stopped dead.

As I arched gracefully over the handlebars, I could see sky, then ground, then sky. I was surprised as anyone, when I landed on my feet. The distraught owner, in the back, had his hands clamped to each side rail. He was sprawled across the seat and hanging on for dear life. He was unhurt, but seemed to be half in and half out of the ditch, when all motion stopped.

We were alive, but I had one very upset Formosan who was wringing his hands as he surveyed the bent front wheel of his one and only pedicab. He was uttering a few Chinese words that I don't think complimented my driving techniques. It was time to do some very fast settlement negotiations, and depart before he could draw a crowd that could include the police. Another twenty calmed him enough for me to escape this rapidly growing accident scene. I was out of there and on my way (as a passenger) in another pedicab before he could say Chiang Kai-shek.

My competitors were at the finish line, drinks in hand, waiting to present me with the tab. They had no sympathy, I had saved the United States from a major international incident, and they still wanted me to pay. No gratitude at all. I sure hope those two little kids appreciated my sacrifice.

By-the-way, I gave up pedicab racing, it seemed I had much more control when I was in the cockpit of a single engine jet fighter at thirty thousand feet. The pedestrian traffic is certainly minimal at that level, and there isn't a drainage ditch that can be seen for miles! I thought about giving up martinis too, but let's not go overboard, only one resolve at a time is all a body can stand.

"A Thousand and One"

The dart, a four winged, delta shaped, aluminum covered target, was fairly new to the tactical fighter force. It had been accepted as the new aerial training target to replace the old tried and true banner. Tow ships, with the banner, normally maintained a straight and level flight path. With the dart, it could maneuver in flight and the dart would take the same flight path as the towship. This presented the attacking aircraft with increased firing angles that were more representative of an enemy aircraft's tactics. It had been used during the '58 Fighter Weapons Meet and was slowly becoming the target for all fighter units in the field.

Mike, my old buddy from many years back, and I had been experts on all phases of the dart target system. We could assemble, launch, and fire at it. We could take it from the crate to the towship, build it up, wind the cable, and make it work just like it had been designed from the drawing board. While we were at Nellis, we had visited all the stateside gunnery teams prior to the gunnery meet to instruct on the intricacies of operations and maintenance. Now we were at Clark Air Base in the Philippines, assigned to the 510th Fighter Squadron. They had never used the dart target before. All the equipment was in place, they just hadn't put it together or even tried to utilize it in their training program. Guess who got the job of trying to make it work? Mike and I were the volunteers(?).

The squadron had been concentrating on air-to-ground weapon deliveries. The air-to-air portion had not been a mandatory requirement for the past several years. New training requirements changed all of that. The fighter units in the Far East Air Forces were instructed to meet all phases of tactical fighter weapons delivery modes. This meant getting qualified on the air-to-air dart target, as well as continuing the air-to-ground requirements that had previously been part of their training program.

Everyone was looking forward to having something new, the hooker was working out a new drop procedure, and getting it approved by the Base Operations people. They controlled what occurred around the field when it came to target drops and such. The old banners could be dropped from a low altitude with acceptable accuracy. The dart had to be dropped from above 1500 feet to allow a retarding parachute to ease its descent to the ground. At that altitude, wind could cause the target to drift, so there was a chance the cable could end up across the runway or outside the normal target drop zone. Timing for the release point was critical.

The base operations officer wasn't your 'easy to work with' type, especially if he was dealing with two subordinate Captains. He was very wary of any new or different device that was to be used on his airdrome. It became Mike's and my problem to get a workable procedure approved and cleared through an all powerful, Major Wallace. Half the UN Charter could have been worked out with less negotiation. We could have been an enemy bombing force, and gotten better cooperation for an attack on the field.

How would we know when to drop the target?....How would we line up properly with the drop zone?....Suppose the target didn't come off?.....What if someone was in the drop zone?...Who?... Where?...When?...What?...It went on for at least twenty questions or more! We worked and reworked every detail. There was an "i" that needed dotting, the spacing on the drop zone diagram wasn't to scale, and we hadn't spelled "Bullshot" correctly! We had used an 'i' in shot! (How could that of happened?)

We were about to get approval to launch our first dart target. Everything was ready for the Major's signature on a document just under the size and breadth of the Manhattan phone book. When he asked, "How will you know when three seconds are up after you pass the initial point (IP) for drop?" "Well," we said, "we will count one...,two...,three..., and drop." From the look on his face, that answer was somewhere miles short of total acceptability. "No, no, no," he said with the screech of a barnyard owl, "you must count..., a thousand and one..., a thousand and two..., a thousand and three..., and then drop." Get serious! Why not use a stop watch? (That thought was left unsaid, in the interest of time and career development) We bowed and scraped, added the one thousand and etc., and were off to fly some darts.

We were up and away on a glorious day. The sky was a bright blue, the sun a golden ball, and there wasn't a cloud to mar the horizon. I was the towee for the first flight, and Mike the shootee. The dart launched just like we said it would, things were going as we had briefed. It was almost, as we had written it down for the Major. We proceeded to the air-to-air range area and commenced our scheduled firing mission. Mike made passes at the dart until he ran out of ammunition, getting hits on each and every pass. The dart performed as advertised, it was a successful first attempt from all aspects, now back to the field to drop and debrief.

I called the tower for dart drop clearance, I could almost feel the good Major up there waiting for me to start the countdown. The tower cleared me without asking how I would know when three seconds had transpired. I had expected a rehearsal, but I guess the tower operator was giving me the benefit of the doubt. All the switches were set for drop. I passed the IP and counted to three, my way (who was to know?), and hit the pickle button. Nothing happened! It didn't come off! What was wrong with this perfect mission? Mike was on my wing and confirmed that the target was still trailing behind. "Let's try it again, I will recycle the switches," was my flabbergasted comment. The tower cleared me for the re-drop, I was expecting the Major to ask me if I had messed up the count.

I retraced the very exacting pattern, being careful not to cut any corners with my Base Op friends watching. I aligned properly with the drop zone, I recounted as I passed the IP, I depressed the pickle button; Nothing! The same result, the target failed to disengage.

By this time, fuel was becoming a problem for me. I had just enough to go to the ground range, drag the target off by letting it hit the ground, then return for a landing. Mike was sticking right with me. He confirmed that the target detached from the tow cable when it hit the ground within the range complex, and that there was some undetermined amount of cable left behind me. Just how much, he wasn't sure, but not enough to bother anything. (That was his estimate). Fuel was down to a bare minimum, it was a certainty that I was going to land some place, hopefully it would be Clark Field.

I knew there was some amount of cable behind, so my plan was to make my approach to the runway as steep as possible, and land a little long. That way, the cable wouldn't hit short and cause any damage. It was a good plan, the only problem was that Mike had grossly underestimated the amount of a cable remaining. I didn't know that, but I was still attempting to minimize whatever damage there might be. I was trying to time my approach to miss over flying the steady stream of vehicular traffic that was constantly on the base's perimeter road. I was hoping to hit a gap between cars in case the cable came dragging across the highway. This was the main road that led to the main gate, and it was always busy, no matter what time of day it was. I thought I was going to be lucky, no school buses or little old ladies were in sight as I flashed over the busy thoroughfare and settled down past the runway's threshold. I whipped by in what seemed to be a perfect traffic window. As far as I was concerned, everything, with the exception of the on-base drop, had gone according to plan.

Whipped by was an understatement, whipped up would have been more appropriate. The tower did comment to me on the Ground Control frequency as I was taxing to the parking area, that there seem to be some sort of traffic tic-up on the base highway. The Major from Base Ops was at the parking area, pacing back and forth in front of my intended slot. The heat from under his collar was almost visible. He was yelling up to me before I could complete parking my aircraft. It might be said that, he was a bit over exercised. I also think, his damage estimate was a little exaggerated. It wasn't twelve cars and four dozen runway approach light stands that were demolished. In truth, the cable had torn the fender off a passing car. It had been an old car, and the driver had not been injured, just surprised. Also, there had been a little damage to some landing and threshold lights short of the runway, but only twenty-two.. A shed, housing some of the electronic gear for the approach system, didn't have a roof any more, plus a couple of other incidental items that slip my mind at this time. The Major was threatening court martial, burning at the stake, a firing squad, or all three. For sure, there would be no more darts from his (?) airfield if he had anything to say about it!

Mike, having landed before me, was standing well back from the scene. He seemed patient to wait until the fireworks had calmed down before he decided to come over and help determine the cause of our problem. He said later, that he didn't want to get in the way of any stray bullets that the Major might spray around.

After an intensive investigation; the time it took for me to get out of the cockpit, the Major to wind down, and Mike and I to go under the wing; we found we had a faulty solenoid in the release mechanism. It wouldn't open when the pickle button was depressed, therefore the cable remained firmly attached to the aircraft. After the solenoid was replaced, and checked several times, we were ready to continued the dart program at Clark Air Base. The Major wasn't really a big

137

supporter of the continuance, but it seemed that the Wing Commander felt that the mission requirements slightly overshadowed the Base Operations Officer's desires.

I really feel that Major Wallace's happiest day, was when Mike and I departed Clark. We never damaged any additional base or runway accessories. Traffic, on the main highway, was never slowed or interrupted again when we were landing or taking off. There just seemed to be some slight misgiving whenever we came in contact with him. There was one other time when we were making low passes off the approach end of the runway. We were simulating strafing runs to cover paratroopers that had just landed. He felt that our flight paths were in conflict with safe clearance to portions of the base. But, we explained that we were in support of a major joint exercise that he had been fully aware of, and approved. A stand-off at best.

The only way that I can explain his concern is, he never truly trusted how we arrived at a three count. Funny, how some little thing like that will stick in a person's mind. I know I'll never forget, he made a believer out of me, for at least, a thousand and one,... a thousand and two,... seconds or so!

"Sometimes It's Easier to Buy a Drink"

The occasions were limited when we flew into Kadena Air Base, on the island of Okinawa. However, when we did, it always meant some good flying competition, against some top-notch pilots. It also presented an excuse for some world-class partying when the days activities ended. The 18th Fighter Wing at Kadena was equipped with three squadrons of F-100 Supersabres. Kadena, halfway between the Philippines and Japan, was one of the mainstay bases of the US Air Forces stationed in the Far East. This meant they were three times as large as our lone 510th tactical fighter squadron in the Philippines. While outnumbered numerically, we were able to hold our own in the flying events. Each event was flown on an equal basis. The competitions were based strictly on how well each pilot delivered his bombs and rockets. Strafing was also an event, with each hole in the target counting a point for the team. We would usually have a three day competition, with about six aircraft participating from each unit. We needed mostly clear weather for a good competition, for it could be a factor that limited our conventional weapons deliveries. On a previous and memorable occasion, weather did almost shut our contest down.

Our Wing Director of Operations (DO), Colonel "Bull" H., had led us to Okinawa on this previous excursion, which happened to be during a particularly rainy time of year. Bull wasn't your average Colonel. He had all the proper qualities, they just didn't always mesh correctly. On our first few days after arrival, the airbase was completely socked-in with rain. That meant, there was very little chance of getting any fruitful flying accomplished on the gunnery ranges. Each day, we would accompany Col. "Bull" to the weather station to talk to the weather forecaster. It was always the same story, 'maybe it will be better tomorrow'. After each extensive briefing, the Colonel would always stop to scan the weather radar screen. He studied it as if he was a swami, about to tell someone's fortune. He would ponder, and scratch his head, as the sweeping probe made a couple of cycles. Then, he would make his same comment, "Where did all this Fu_____ rain come from?" He would then storm out of the weather office, making some very unkind remarks about weather people, in general.

After several days of this, the forecaster had just about all he could stand, from this less-than-knowledgeable individual. Finally, he got the nerve to say, "Sir, that isn't rain, it's ground clutter!" So much for "Bull's" radar scope interpretation course. Naturally, "Bull" couldn't let it go at that. His parting blast was, "If it's ground clutter, how come all that rain is outside?" You must admit, that our senior officer had logic on his side.

On this particular occasion, the weather was good, and luckily for us, our weather guru stayed home. I was leading six aircraft and an equal number of pilots. It was our intention to have a small gunnery competition with our friends from the 18th Wing. It would be the Filipinos against the Okinawans. It must be remembered that Kadena was also the home base of my old and true friend, Fire Can Dan. Dan was a mainstay in the 18th Fighter Wing. He always made a name for himself, wherever he went, however sometimes it couldn't be said aloud in proper company. It was always nice to renew old friendships, plus get some really good flying on an unfamiliar weapons range. I also knew that we could expect some jovial times, after flying terminated, with Fire Can and his sidekick, Purcy. The Stag Bar, in the Kadena Officer's Club, was always jumping when these two were in residence.

The following day had been a fighter pilot's dream, good flying, and decent weather. All the range missions went as planned. The scores were very acceptable for both competing teams. We seemed to have our skills sharpened, if and when, we ever needed to really beat up on some unscrupulous enemy. (Little did we know at the time, that such was only a few years away). That evening, the Stag Bar was jumping. The beer and sodas were being consumed, and the competition was continuing on the ping-pong table and shuffle board. People were rolling dice at the bar or lagging pucks on the shuffle board for drinks—common ways to joust for the libation of your choice. The volume of talk was louder than the roar of the day's jet engine noise. Fire Can, Purcy, and I were in a deep conversation at the end of the bar. We were just sipping a few beers and minding our business, when one of my fighter jocks sauntered up.

Now, this troop might have been just one story short of having his elevator go all the way to the top of his building. He could fly fighters, but sometimes his judgment was questionable—at best. And this was one of the times. He had been trying to engage Fire Can Dan in conversation for a major part of the evening, but Dan had been shrugging him off. The troop, I'll call Sammy, would go away for a while, but like the sands of time, he would return, almost on the hour. He was getting to the obnoxious mode. His intrusions were less than appropriate, even for a stag bar atmosphere. Comments like, "What makes you think you're such hot stuff, Tin Can?" Also, "How did you learn to fly, 'Hot Shot', by correspondence?" Luckily, Fire Can was in good spirits, or Sammy would have needed to insure that his Blue Cross hospital plan was paid up. Finally, he resorted to a more direct approach. He barged in between Dan and me, and confronted Dan head-on. "I'll roll you for a drink, Hot Shot!" he said.

I think the second 'Hot Shot', hit a nerve. Dan immediately said, "No, let's flip for one." Before my fearless (and slightly surprised), young fighter pilot could say a word, Fire Can spun around on his bar stool, reached down, and grabbed Sammy by his foot. Without so much as 'Are you ready', he physically tossed him up into the air. The flip sent him head over heels crashing to the floor. It could have only been scored a "1" on a scale of 1 to 10 for what resembled a full spinning, one and three quarter, somersault dive.

Before Sammy could recover, Dan reached down, and grabbed him by the back of his collar, and the seat of his pants. "You, want to flip again? No, then how about lagging for one?" All that was heard was a groan. Before Sammy could agree, deny, or depart, Dan had him airborne, again. In an instant, Sammy was sliding, face down, along the shuffle board. He would have gone off the far end of the board, but gratefully, he hung up in the scoring apparatus mid-way down the slide. "Maybe now, you want to flip again?" Dan said, as he started towards the mid-point of the board to retrieve Sammy's grotesque body.

"Whoa, stop, cease," I said. "I might need this troop to fly tomorrow." Sammy looked like he had just been saved from the jaws of death. Perhaps he had!

Maybe it was the stark look in Sammy's eyes; or just the pathetic figure of a half bent body laying on the shuffle board; or me saying 'Enough'. But to everyone's amazement, Dan walked slowly over to Sammy, and patted him on the head. He looked at him a little sadly, and said, "*Let me*, buy *you* a drink." I think the most surprised person in the place was Sammy.

Sammy was heard to say later, "Gee, I only wanted to be his pal." I, and most everyone in the place, thought he had an odd way of going about it. Sometimes it seems to take some people a little longer to get that elevator all the way up to the top floor! In Sammy's case, I doubt it will ever make it.

I guess you could say, it was just a run-of-the-mill night in the Kadena O' Club Stag Bar. A few friends flipping or lagging on the shuffle board for a few drinks. It's those sentimental memories that bring back those good old days. In Sammy's case, it was more than likely a slight case of stupidity and certainly more than his share of sore body parts.

Maybe next time, the bartender could think of a number?

"Party Time"

The period between Christmas and New Year's Eve seemed to bring out the party spirit in the 510th fighter troops. There were other times during the year, like Spring, Summer, or Fall that also aroused those festive juices, but the Yule Season far out did any of those. The weather in the Philippines during that time of year was balmy and nice. So, outside partying was the norm, rather than having to stay inside like you would in the States. The snow was lacking, but that was the only thing. The revelry was as lively, and gala as any ever seen in other parts of the world. The only drawback was, the entire squadron couldn't be completely soused at any one time. This meant the party schedule had to be sequenced through the flights. It was a must to keep a few clear heads, just in case someone was called on to fly. Also, the alert status had to be maintained up North. So in reality, only about half the squadron could be less than sober at any one time. It was probably a blessing, I don't think that Clark Air Base could have contained the entire unit in an all out blast. We could have produced a 3 point 8 on the Richter scale, with only seventy-five percent participating. The entire unit would have rivaled the San Francisco fiasco of old.

Usually, the initial embryo would come to life in, or around, the Fullam house. Wayne was the instigator of more parties than any other individual in the squadron. He was an outstanding fighter pilot, who had a gift of making people enjoy themselves. He and his wife, Boonçey, were the type of couple that every squadron needed. They kept everyone congenial, and in a friendly mode. Sometimes guys get a bit testy when stationed a long way from home, and the Philippine Islands certainly qualified as being miles and miles from home. So, when the Fullams started a bash, it was usually a good one. Many times, frozen daiquiris would be the drink of choice. Wayne would use food coloring to keep track of which round of drinks each person was on. The rules were, you couldn't have consecutive drinks of the same color. It made for a rainbow of glasses, with tongues to match.

This Christmas Eve party, however, was different. It did start at the Fullams, it did consist of mostly "D" Flight troops, but it gathered momentum from there. It had started earlier in the day, with just a portion of the "D" Flight people. Some neighbors, not even in the 510th, had joined in and were part of the parade when they came around the corner headed for Mike's place. Mike was their flight commander, and lived directly across the street from me. Their mission was to serenade Mike, on this eve of Christmas. By the time they arrived, the spontaneous gaggle was somewhat less than orderly. Several were carrying a completely decorated Christmas tree, one troop had a bugle which he blew from time to time, others were transporting bottles of booze with an unnamed concoction, and a jolly Santa Claus was pulling a little red wagon. The wagon contained Dumpy D, one of "D" Flight's finest. He was sprawled, flat on his back, hands dragging along the pavement, completely passed out. He had been at the party's birth, and they weren't about to leave him out of the finale.

The carol serenade on Mike's lawn, left a lot to be desired. It was certainly a long way from the Mormon Tabernacle Choir. More of a cross between cows mooing, and a couple of love sick moose baying in the woods. The final touch gave it just that little bit of cheer, that brought the Yuletime spirit closer to home. Someone dressed in an elf outfit, began dancing around the group, tossing soap flakes in the air to simulate snow. It was really touching in the 80 degree heat and the 100% humidity. Finally, the crowd faded away, leaving only the bent tinseled tree, and Dumpy D in his wagon, fast asleep. The perfect start to the Christmas party season.

New Year's Eve however, was the real culmination to the parties. We were at the Officer's Club, on the patio, for a beautiful evening under the stars. The place was jammed, but the other members of the 510 squadron had commandeered two large tables on the edge of the dance floor. The patio was surrounded by a curved roof that gave the impression of an old Greek courtyard. Only the back row of tables were under the narrow overhang. We were, maybe, ten yards from the inner edge of the roof. The evening was well into its full crescendo.

My old squadron commander from Nellis, John H. had joined us. He was on temporary duty from Pacific Air Force Headquarters, visiting the 13th Air Force Headquarters, located on Clark Air Base. It was an odd time to be away from home, but John was a bachelor, so I guess any place, with friends, was fine. He was a full Colonel, and had a good reputation in the fighter world. He was a party animal, and he had come to the right place. The occasion called for a toast of champagne.

Hurrah for Colonel John....! To really put an exclamation to the toast, we all tossed our glasses onto the top of the tin roof overhang. (There wasn't a fireplace into which we could fling our glasses like the knights of old.) The noise almost stopped the dancers, they thought the cymbal player had dropped his instrument. The tinkle of glass carried nicely on such a starlit night. After the second round, my wife thought it was such a good idea, that she again, tossed her glass. (She was a traditionalist.) Unfortunately her throw didn't make the overhang, it splattered, dead in the middle of the table behind us. It took several apologies before we could calm things down, and reclaim our normal drinking stride. Almost, but not quite; Lt. Colonel Larry P., my current squadron commander, staggered up to our table and said, "The next person that throws a glass will be kicked out of here." The silence was deafening. Why should he be so upset with our endeavors? He wasn't even at our table. I was on my way to speak to him when, a resounding crash of a glass hitting the roof, broke the silence. Spinning around to see who had tempted fate, I caught a glimpse of Col. John holding his follow through, from what must have been a perfect toss. Larry P. was beside himself, he spun away from the table and pulled me with him.

He stopped right in the middle of the dance floor, and proceeded to read me the riot act. He blamed me for the entire disruption. I certainly had a hand in some of the proceedings, but certainly not the entire thing. Here it was only ten o'clock, two hours till the New Year, and I was almost ready to be kicked out of one of the best parties of the year. He said, "If one more glass is thrown, or any other disturbance comes from *your* table, I will hold you personally responsible. Is that clear?" My only answer was, "Yes Sir, yes sir, and a final, YES SIR"! I would talk to him tomorrow; tonight, I was going to bring in the New Year. When I returned to the table, I thanked Col. John for almost ending my young career. He smiled, and said, "Don't worry, it will take a lot more than a broken glass to slow you down." It must have calmed me for the time, for it really became a great evening, to almost remember.

The next day, at a "get well" Brunch, and after a good night's sleep, Larry P. came up to me and said, "Hope you had a good time last night Dan, it sure was a nice party."..... Shades of early Alzheimer's!....... So went the parties at dear old Clark, there would surely be something to celebrate in a day or two. We could hardly wait!

145

"What White Panel?"

General Theodore Milton, had just been assigned as the new Commander of 13th Air Force. It meant he would receive his second star, a nice move up the ladder in this man's air force. His previous assignment had been in 5th Air Force in Japan. He had become a fighter pilot's general, although his background had been in the big ugly fellows (BUFF's). It went way back to the big raids on the oil fields during WW II. He had led his force through, when others failed. He was a true combat leader, one that you would want to follow regardless of the situation. His fighter experience was minimal, but he had been in the process of completing his checkout in the F-100 when he received his new assignment. His theory was; to have a good feel for the mission, you needed a thorough knowledge of the equipment. That way, he would be in a better position to achieve the goals and missions of the air forces in the Far East.

Except for the F-100 checkout, most of his fighter time had been in interceptors. The F-102 was the air defense mainstay in the Far East and the general would spend most of his flying hours in that century series bird. That meant he would be flying with our sister squadron, the 509th, since they were equipped with F-102's and their mission was air defense.

However, one of his first priorities upon reaching Clark Air Base, was to complete his familiarity with the F-100. It had been sometime since his last F-100 flight, so he could be a little rusty. He would fly with our squadron, the 510th purple tailed screaming falcons, to get back up to speed. And I had been designated to serve as his IP. Now, it didn't bother me that I would be flying with a general. He probably knew more about airplanes than our entire group of squadron pilots put together. His aide, a F-100 instructor qualified pilot himself, didn't want to take this initial flight at Clark. He felt the general should fly with squadron personnel and he didn't want to deprive us of letting the general see us first hand. I didn't have much time to worry about it, since his first flight was scheduled for the next morning. I couldn't wait.

The day was bright and cheery, it was a perfect day for flying. I had everything ready for the briefing, when I heard the building being called to attention. It was the norm when a general officer entered the operations area. He had arrived! I was all set, but I wasn't expecting the spectacle that entered my door. In walked one of the most impressive officers I had ever seen. Tall, and distinguished, just what every general should look like. I was almost at a loss for words. My first statement was almost a disaster, I said, "Sir, I guess we had better spend more time on the flying techniques of a real fighter plane. You probably have the straight and level interceptor techniques perfected." There was a very significant pause. He looked at me with a very penetrating stare, before saying, "I guess you are correct, Captain. We don't spend much time upside down in 102's. His stern glare slowly faded into the slightest of smirks. Who was this young upstart, seemed to be his question. He said, "Let's brief, I'm ready to fly." I felt like I may have just dodged a bullet, he could have finished my career on the spot for that bit of impertinence.

The flight went well. That is to say, we did all the loops and rolls available and made it up and down, all in one piece. It was evident he enjoyed taking the SuperSabre through its paces. He could pull "G's" with the best and seemed to feel at home right side up or upside down. His eyes were sparkling the minute we climbed down in the parking area. When I asked if he wanted to try another flight soon, he was ready to go immediately. During the debrief, he expressed a desire to fire the guns. He said he had never fired guns from a fighter, and would like to give it a try. Who was I to deny such a request? He was the big boss, and if he wanted to shoot the guns, load up all four.

About two days later, we were all set for a go at the ground range in Crow Valley. The range consisted of a 300 foot bombing circle, six strafing targets, and a red and white control panel. The bombing circle could be scored by a triangulation device, which gave miss distance from the center of the circle. The strafing targets were 20x20 foot panels with a large black bull's-eye in the upper half of the frame. The control panel could be flipped from red to white, depending on whether an aircraft was cleared to make a live firing pass. White for firing, red for no-fire. It was a small but efficient setup, and was virtually our private place to use as our mission requirements dictated.

Since it was the General's first hot firing mission on the range, we spent a lot of time briefing on range procedures, and minimum safe altitudes. We only planned to strafe on this mission, so considerable time was spent on the target set-up, and the gunnery pattern in particular. The bombs would be left to another time. From the backseat, I wouldn't have the best forward visibility. I would only be able to see the sides of the target, the exact aim point of the guns, could only be seen by General Milton. He alone could see the exact impact of our lethal stream of lead when he depressed the trigger on the control stick. It should be a piece of cake.

It was another pleasant day on the tropical sunlit island of Luzon. The rich green jungle growth that bordered the range area, made the stark white targets stand out like a row of teeth, marred only by the black bull's-eyes that dotted each upper portion. We were cleared on to the range, it was ours to rip and tear as we pleased. We could take our time, we weren't in any hurry to pulverize the surrounding area. When the F-100 guns are fired, the empty cartridges are ejected overboard. They fall to the ground along the run-in path of the aircraft. It was the practice at the Crow Valley range, to allow the small native people (Negritos), to collect these brass cartridge shells. In turn, they provided protection for the range complex during the non-use hours. They were allowed onto the range after the aircraft had completed their firing passes. During the firing passes, they would crouch down behind the red and white control panel. Safe enough(?), from steely eyed combat fighter pilots pressing to disintegrate the black bull's-eye on each and every pass.

Today however, was a different story. We made several dry passes towards the targets. This allowed the general to get the feel of diving this silver machine towards the ground at 400 knots. He was having a great time. When he reached the foul line (1000 feet short of the targets), he would apply the necessary "G's" to pull the aircraft safely up and away, getting positioned for another pass. He had made ten or so dry passes at the #1 target, the one positioned several yards to the right of the red and white control panel. All appeared to be straight and true. He seemed to have the touch. Now, we were ready to put some holes in that white sheet of cloth. I called the range control officer, and told them we would be "HOT" on the next pass. We made a smooth gentle turn on to the final run-in. The general called, "In, Hot, and White." Meaning that the control panel was white (cleared to fire), and that our gun switch had been pushed up to "Fire." We were ready to push some lead.

I told him I would attempt to line us up with the target on the first pass and he could pull the trigger. As we rolled out, the nose of the aircraft should have been in the vicinity of the #1 target. I said, "Ease the pipper up and give it a good burst." We were approaching at a rapid rate on a slight angle from a straight run-in, but it was close enough for 'government work.' I was straining to make sure we were aligned properly. Just as we approached firing range, I could see I had pointed the nose at the white control panel instead of the #1 target. "DON'T..." Burrrrrrrrrrup went the guns! "FIRE!".... My warning was ripped apart by a healthy dose of 20 millimeter ammunition. Uh Oh!..... As we pulled off the target, I was able to look back and see about ten Negritos looking like a covey of quail being flushed from a thicket. "Well General, seems we got some hits in the control panel, and sent some of our little native friends scampering for new cover." Such a minor mishap didn't deter us. General Milton continued our mission and made several effective firing passes on the correct target without having me interfere. He put bullets in the panel on each pass until we finally ran out of ammunition.

The result of our first pass were: we put eleven holes in the white panel, two Negritos refused to return to Crow Valley for several weeks, and four others never would get close to the white control panel until all aircraft had departed the range area. Apparently brass shell casings weren't bringing top dollar on the local market during that period, or at least not enough to risk the safety (?) of the 'White Panel!'

The General waited a few weeks before he continued his gunnery missions. Seems like he was satisfied with strafing, now on to bigger and better bombs! Let's put some bombs in that orange pylon—too bad Vietnam was still a couple years away!

"Slightly Bent or Totally Destroyed?"

Charlie S. was leading the flight of four, it was his final checkout to achieve flight lead status. He was a big guy, heavy shoulders, and built like a linebacker. He had played varsity ball for either Minnesota or Wisconsin, and looked like he could still make the team. He had briefed the mission as a low level navigation round robin, it would end with a simulated nuclear weapons delivery on the air-to-ground range in Crow Valley. The day was clear and shiny, just like so many in the Philippines. It was a super day to be alive, and to be flying. Our nav route would take us out over the crystal blue of the South China Sea, and bring us back over the stark green jungle, that covered the mountains of Luzon, the main island of the Philippine chain.

We had started engines, and were approaching the number one position for take-off. Sammy was Charlie's wingman, and would be on his right wing for the formation take-off. Sammy had recovered from his bout with Fire Can Dan in Okinawa, and was attempting to prove his aviation prowess. I was in the backseat of a tandem seated F-100F, checking out Bill W. as element lead. We had Tom K. on our wing, which completed the four ship flight. Both Bill and Tom were proven fighter jocks, and could be counted on to do more than their share on any type mission. The tower cleared us for take-off as we rolled into our line up position on the runway. We had briefed for ten seconds spacing between elements, so when the lead element released brakes and lit their afterburners, we held our position for the required separation. On the dot, Bill released our brakes and engaged the burner. He gave Tom a head nod for each, enabling him to maintain perfect wing position. We were rolling as one.... when: Suddenly, there was a wall of smoke and fire directly in front of us. Bill's reaction was instantaneous, he pulled the power back to idle and braked us to a crawl. He used the radio to alert Tom. What had happened? The flame and smoke died down almost as quickly as it had flared. It definitely hadn't been an airplane that ignited. There were various size pieces of metal on the runway, but the two lead aircraft could be seen up ahead, just getting airborne. Apparently, an external fuel tank had come off one of the lead element's aircraft. But which one, and had it done any serious damage when it torched off directly in our take-off path?

Charlie was asking Sammy if his airplane was handling properly. Sammy replied in the affirmative. We were trying to listen to their conversation and pick our way through the jagged pieces of metal that had been left on the runway. We didn't want to puncture our tires, because we still expected to get airborne as soon as the runway was cleared. Once we got past the debris, the lead element's situation began to unfold.

Just as they had rotated for take-off, Charlie's right external fuel tank had departed his aircraft and banged into Sammy's left main landing gear. They had continued their take-off, which was fortunate, because there hadn't been enough runway remaining to abort. Sammy was instructed to leave his landing gear in the down position, and climb to a higher altitude before checking his aircraft for stability. Fuel wasn't a problem, and we wanted to assess the situation before we arrived at a plan of action.

Bill and I taxied back to the parking area, and changed seats. I wanted to be in the front cockpit, in order to have positive control when we went up to inspect Sammy's landing gear. From the information that Charlie was passing down, there was more than just a little damage.

We were back in the take-off position, just as the runway was cleared of debris. Elapsed time couldn't have been over ten minutes. We had immediate clearance for take-off, and wasted no time in blasting off to join up with Sammy. They were at ten thousand feet, directly over the base, so we were there in seconds. Sammy was maintaining 180 knots, with his gear in the down position. His gear indicator still showed, down and locked. It was decided to leave it that way, rather than risk fouling it more by trying to cycle it up and down. He had tested the aircraft at near stall speed, without evidence of any unusual flight characteristics. It appeared that, except for the damaged left main gear, he had no problem until landing time arrived. The question was: Would his landing gear hold up when he touched down on the runway?

I moved in under his aircraft to get as close a look as possible. If I could have opened my canopy, I could have touched his left main gear. The gear appeared to be in place, but it wasn't without damage. One of the bracing rods was bent, the gear door had a large piece torn away, and there were gouges along the under side of the wing. The main cylinder, that locked the gear in the down position, appeared fully extended. But, there were some deep marks on the cylinder case from the impact of the fuel tank. It was difficult to estimate just what would occur when, and if, he tried to land. All of this was being discussed on the air with the maintenance people on the ground. There was no solid conclusion from any quarter. After, several minutes of this, Sammy finally piped up and said, "Maybe it would be best if I bailed out"! His voice was less than firm, in fact, it was somewhat high pitched. I had the instinct impression that he was beginning to contemplate the consequences of trying to land that wounded bird. I really couldn't blame him, for no one could guarantee what might happen when the landing gear hit the runway. But, whether he liked it or not, we weren't going to let him leap out. Even a bent aircraft from a crash landing, was better than a smoking hole in the ground. A minor accident was a lot better than a major, which would be the case if he ejected. We could fix a partially wounded Super Sabre. Sammy's choices were narrowed to one, the powers-to-be voted for a landing.

Sammy needed to burn down some of his fuel load. The plan was to have minimum on board when he landed, just in case the aircraft skidded to an unusual stop. If that occurred, we didn't want Sammy to become a bonfire, it could ruin his whole day. Sammy was trying hard to keep his courage up, he asked me if I wanted to land ahead of him in case his gear did fold. He said that the runway might be blocked, which could run me short on fuel. It was a very nice thought. I said, "No sweat, I have more than enough fuel, they will have plenty of time to scrape you up before I need to land." He coughed or gagged! It hadn't come out exactly the way I intended, "I mean, regardless what happens Sammy, I'll have sufficient airborne time before I need to land. Thanks anyway." He was getting anxious to get on with it, and I couldn't fault that. It is very tiring, flying around at slow speed with the gear down. The F-100 Super Sabre was meant to go fast, not hang just above stall speed, burning fuel for nothing. We were on our fifteenth orbit of the field, when finally, Sammy's fuel gauge hit the bingo mark. He was ready to give it a try.

The red fire equipment had been positioned adjacent to the runway, they were ready to cover any unexpected situation. We were on final approach for landing. I was on Sammy's left, in a loose wing position so that I could get a good look at the left main gear when it touch the runway. Sammy was holding a steady descent, he was doing his best to make as smooth a touchdown as possible. The moment of truth had arrived! The tires kissed the concrete approach end of the runway, skipped slightly, and Sammy's left main gear slowly wavered in the air. It looked like a quivering twig that had just been snapped off it's mother branch;.......the gear was going to collapse!

"Sammy, it didn't hold," I yelled. "Hang on and don't eject, the crash equipment is right with you." His wing came down, making contact with the runway. The aircraft started a rotation to the left, causing the right gear to fold. It continued to spin off the runway, spewing sod and dirt in its wake. As I went by, Sammy's canopy came off and up in a spiraling motion. It reminded me of a child's top, spinning out of control when it is yanked to hard. I held my breath, hoping it wouldn't be followed by the seat....... It wasn't.......! Sammy hung tight, and rode the spinning machine to it's grinding, lurching stop. It appeared to be one of the most fascinating carnival whirligigs that could be imagined.

There was no fire, Sammy had shut off his engine at touchdown, which stopped the fuel to the engine. The crash crew was immediately on the scene, and had him out and safe before the dust had barely settled.

Things had gone according to plan; the aircraft was only partly bent, there wasn't a big gaping hole to be covered, and the pilot was *hardly* any the worse for wear. Sammy was a little reluctant to make any formation take-offs for awhile, but I guess that was to be expected. Also, he seemed to spend more time examining his leader's aircraft during pre-flight inspections, than his own. In fact, he was a big advocate for single ship take-offs for some years to come. I wonder why?

"The Aussies Are Coming"

The practice of exchange rotations between fighter units produced very profitable training periods, particularly when it included our Allies the Australians. The 77th Squadron, stationed at Butterworth in Malaysia, was one of the best and we looked forward to our reciprocal visits, either at Butterworth or Clark. They were equipped with a souped up version of the Sabrejet which the Canadians had perfected from the US version. It had a super Rolls Royce engine and flight characteristics that put it in the class of our F-100 Super Sabre. Each time we met, we learned a lot about using our equipment with an unfamiliar adversary, training that would pay dividends if we got into another shooting war. Also, the Australians were some of the most gregarious people I've ever run into. I had gotten to know some of them when the 77th was on the opposite side of the field at Kimpo, Korea. They were partying people then, and nothing had happened to change that aspect of their demeanor.

A visit was due, and the Aussies were on their way to Clark Field in the Philippine Islands. Batten down all the wine cellars, call in the young kids and small girls, and get ready for some super flying and late night partying. We had learned our lesson the last time we shared their hospitality. We found it a bit difficult to drink to the wee hours of the morning, and then fly three maximum performance missions the next day. They had literally worn us down, hardly giving us a chance to get enough sleep to sustain a non-flying type, much less a jet fighter pilot. This time they were in our ball park, and we had to come up with a crafty scheme that would favor the home team.

Arrival day was here. Six bright and shiny Australian Sabres came flashing across the field in perfect formation. They pitched out with precision spacing and touched down only seconds apart. We greeted them as they pulled into the parking slots that had been reserved for their visit. Each pilot was handed a cool beer as soon as his canopy rolled back and there was a second waiting for him by the time he descended to the ramp. We wanted to get things started off on the right foot. They were being led by an old friend I had known in Korea, Squadron Leader Mike Gammon. He was the epitome of the

Aussie fighter pilot. His wide and bushy mustache spread across a smiling face that only his mother could love. He looked like he was part of the 'Outback' rolled into the breadth of a six foot frame. A handsome man, if I do say so myself. I can recall his account of identifying a Mig from an F-86 in Korea. He claimed that he was a bit laxed on aircraft recognition so he said, "When I see a swept winged jet, I just fire a long burst from my 20's at the blighter, if he turns North it's a Mig, and if it turns South it's an F-86." A very simple approach if you weren't flying F-86's. We were just lucky that he didn't hit anyone, but I must admit, he was a likable aborigine, poor shot or not.

The morning after the opening party found everyone fresh and ready to fly. We had a full schedule planned for the entire seven days of their visit. Neither group wanted to waste time, because as I mention earlier, this type of training was something you couldn't buy. It was fly and party, fly and party for six straight days. We gave no quarter either in the flying or in the after hour festivities, but the Aussies were certainly holding their own. You could say they really had staying power. They were flying every mission with outstanding results, they were meeting every party formation with the zest of true drinkers from 'Dear Old Down Under', and their bloodshot eyes rivaled each glorious sunset. It appeared they could keep up the present pace for as long as was required or be pickled trying.

The flying was superb and lively. The fighter versus fighter portion saw F-100's pulling their pipers up on the tailpipe of an Aussie sabre. The next turn would produce the opposite, with the sabre at six o'clock to the F-100, tucked in nicely for a simulated kill. Five, six, seven 'G's'—track, track, track—then squeeze the trigger. Several good gunnery film frames that would show the possibility of a shoot-down. Watch out! The sabre pilot pulled up and went hard right, we were in a climbing scissors. Who could out pull the other? Minimum airspeed, almost floating as the two aircraft fought to get behind the other into a firing position. Looks as if they would end up in a draw this time. On to the bombing range, 45 degree dive angle, pink bodies being hurdled towards the ground. Down into the dive, piper on the target, pickle the bomb and pull back on the stick. A hard four 'G' pullout to insure ample ground clearance. Over and over, down and up, down and up, each aircraft had six bombs to hurl towards the ground. If a bomb impacted outside of 10 feet, forget it, it wasn't close enough to count. Time after time the wooden pyramid in the center of the bombing circle was smashed into splinters. These types of sorties were just typical of the flying day. When the flying day ended, each pilot's coveralls was soaked with perspiration looking as if he had just stepped out of the shower. This was strenuous stuff, no wonder everyone was ready for a drink or two when the pretty airplanes were put to rest until another day.

The drinking and frivolity was always accompanied by much loud talking and singing. Most often heard were 'Waltzing Matilda' (the Aussie favorite), and 'Sally in the Alley' (an all time sentimental great from Korea). However, each evening usually closed with a game that would test the skill and stamina of both sides. The most popular (we played it every night) was the 'Tunnel of Doom' or 'How to Break Apart the Dining Room Chairs.' It was the top choice of the walking wounded, I guess they were trying to get even. It seemed to put the finishing touch to the culmination of each evening's activities. All available chairs were turned over so the backs were parallel with the floor. They were then pushed together to form a very narrow tunnel. Rugs were used as a covering, so the tunnel was not only narrow, but dark. Each group picked a team of ten members with the rest of the people along the sides holding the tunnel together. The teams started from opposite ends of the tunnel, and the first one to get all ten members out the far end, won. Needless to say, the going got a bit sticky inside the tunnel, but I can say there was no major physical damage or broken bones to any of the participants, which was quite miraculous.

Cunning and craftiness were winning out. As the old saying goes, 'Don't try to get the best of a fox in his own den', or 'The unsuspecting visitor doesn't have a chance'. Our ace in the hole was Captain Wayne Fullam. He was one of our better fighter pilots, but we were sacrificing his aerial expertise for his ability to organize, guide, participate in, and remain upright in any party environment in the world. Our scheme, which we labeled "The Fullam Stratagem," was simple but foolproof(?). We divided our troops into two groups. We had guys that would fly in the morning and party that night. The second group would get their crew rest and be ready for the next day's missions. This way, we had fresh and rested inputs to fly, fly, fly, and party, party, party. If that didn't keep our visitors busy, Wayne was there from start to finish, a familiar face every night of their entire trip.

156

And it was working! The Aussies seemed a little puzzled during the morning flight briefings, but with the eyes they were looking through, it must have been very difficult to recognize even your closest friend. Most of them would answer roll call, then slowly lower their heads to catch a few more winks before having to go out to their aircraft. Those wide awake coffee ads would have been a bust with these guys. We could've had mannequins in our seats, much less a different set of faces every other morning.

Finally, the closing night arrived, flying was over except for their trip home the next morning. We were having one last party which included our wives. It was a bit more demure than the previous evenings. We passed out trophies for various phases of the week's flying, there were an equal amount going to each group. After our short ceremony, Mike arose and stated he would like to make a special presentation. He said, "We may come from 'Down Under', but we know a get even scheme when we see it. Your double teaming effort was outstanding, almost equaling our endeavors on your last visit to Butterworth. Since each of your teams consumed only half the required alcohol, we would like each of them to have an extra bottle of beer." The words were no sooner out of his mouth, when in came the waiters with twenty-four of the largest bottles of beer ever seen. Those Aussies thought of everything.

I guess our foolproof strategy had been a little thin, we had been caught but we had also gotten even. Wayne was still able to stand, although somewhat shakily, he was only about one step from total saturation. And, if the truth be known, the Aussies had reached the edge of their bounds. Some even admitted they may have exceeded their limit, and the next morning only added credence to their condition.

Our less than bright eyed friends from Butterworth were all strapped into their Sabres. Start engine time was only minutes away when word came down that weather was going to be a problem and they might have to extend their trip by two or three days. You could hear the moans from all six cockpits, Mike Gammon's was the loudest. He said, "I surrender and take back everything I've ever said derogatory about you wonderful fellows. Please just let me leave in peace, I can't take another night." As they climbed down with looks of despair, a fast approaching staff car brought the news that the weather situation was clearing, and they would be able to depart as planned. I guess Mike's prayers must have been answered, for within the hour they got their clearance and were off that airpatch before you could say 'Kangaroo', 'Kookaburra', 'Boomerang', or any other Australian word you might fancy.

It had been a ball. We had gotten loads of excellent training and renewed old friendships, plus made a lot of new ones. The Aussies are great people to have on your side. My only concern was, the next exchange would be at Butterworth! Maybe I'll rotate before that time arrives?

"The Right Place at the Right Time?"

The early 60's were the first indication that our involvement in Southeast Asia might be more than just a trip or two to Saigon. We already had a few troops working with the Vietnamese National Air Force(VNAF), but no one that I knew was very conversant on their progress. It wasn't anything we fighter pilots wanted to get involved in, just a few prop jobs and not any real combat action that was public.

Suddenly, that was to change. The Chief of Staff of the USAF, General Lemay, passed through Clark Air Base much like an overnight whirlwind. He had been to South Vietnam to personally evaluate how our advisors to the VNAF were doing. And he didn't like what he found. He said their aggressive attitude couldn't have upset an old ladies tea party. He intended immediate replacement with people who could get the VNAF up and running as a viable combat unit.

Before anyone could assess this move, several experienced fighter jocks that were on the staff's of 13th Air Force, the 405th Fighter Wing, and other wings in the Far East were on their way to South Vietnam as interim advisor replacements. Gen. Lemay hadn't wasted any time in putting some beef in the program to back up his edicts. People like Grady, Tommy K., Garry W., and several others that knew the proper end of the fighter business were in place before the general could get back to Washington. Only us line jocks were spared, but all eyes were taking a more in-depth look towards the possibilities of more than advisory missions in that part of the world. Little did we know what the future held, but for now, if there was to be a shooting war, we wanted to be a part of it.

Within a matter of weeks Grady, Tommy, and Garry were back at Clark. That was a short tour! However, their stint as advisors was curtailed by an over friendly sergeant with a practical joke that literally blew up in everybodies face. Seems he thought a grenade that was supposedly de-bombed, turned out to be the real thing. Needless to say, when it rolled into the cement walled quarters of the advisory compound, our visiting fighter troops were immediately on the move. They said it looked like a covey of quails flushing from deep cover. Garry passed Tommy on the way to a screen door that only opened inward. After those two passed through, the swinging doors were more than multi-directional, they were barely hanging by a hinge. Grady was a little slower and got caught inside when the detonation occurred. He picked up more metal than his share. No one was spared, Garry's and Tommy's wounds were strictly behind them, they were sort of hit going away. None of the hits were life threatening, luckily all were going to recover. Visiting them in the Clark hospital confirmed that their beer consumption had not been impaired. They had no trouble downing the three six packs we smuggled in.

While the grenade incident wasn't the work of the communist movement, things began to heat up in Laos along the Thailand border. This prompted the powers-to-be to deploy fighters to a Thai base for the expressed purpose of providing conventional firepower, if and when required. The 510th, our squadron, got the duty. This meant that we would be covering two alert locations, the nuclear one on Formosa and now this conventional one in Thailand. Not too many jocks or aircraft would be left at the homedrome, but no one was upset, Oh! to be in on the beginning of a War! Only Big Mike, my longtime buddy from Nellis days, and I had been in the Korean fracas. If you are going to train for the real thing, you might as well get some on you if the opportunity presented itself. This thing might not last long enough to get but a few missions. Ha! There weren't any 'Doves' in the 510th TFS, the bird on our airplanes tail was all 'Hawk' with blood in it's eye.

Mike led the first group of aircraft into Takhli Air Base, which was about 100 miles north of Bangkok. Except for a few Thai Air Force T-28s, the base was empty. It was truly like moving into a bare base set-up. If you didn't bring it with you, it wasn't there. There were several greeters and the sign on the base ops tower made sure you were aware of them. "Welcome to Takhli, Home of the King Cobra." It really made you wish you had packed your flute and basket. No one roamed around in the weeds at night. Most everyone was busy consuming that snake ointment elixir being served at the O'Club bar.

After several weeks and a few pilot rotations, things with the Thailand contingent settled into a regular, but dull routine. There was a scramble or two, but those were recalled before any action ensued. Everyone was sure something would happen soon, but just when, was a true unknown. Here we were all set for some experience building combat, and nothing was happening. What was a well meaning young fighter pilot to do?

My tour in the Philippines was quickly drawing to a close as mid-1962 approached. Was this thing going to erupt before I went back Stateside? It certainly seemed that things were settling down, just my luck. The time for departure was here, we were getting on the Pan Am charter headed for California with assignment to Luke AFB in Arizona. The only consolation I got was from the 13th Air Force Commander, he promised me if things heated up to the boiling point before I signed in at Luke, I could return. It wasn't much but it did give me a sense of being wanted.

Well nothing happened, no war in Southeast Asia, not in 1962 anyway. I signed in and went about the business of flying and training some additional F-100 tigers. As history transpired, the Vietnam conflict was another three or four years away. There was a hic-cup from Cuba, when they attempted to flex their missiles, but both of those are other stories. Amazing how fighter pilots always seem to fear they will miss the 'big show'. It's been a plus for this country to have had so many answer that call when it came. I am fully convinced that when the chips are down, fighter types will always be there to back-up any need, large or small.

Keep it up, luckily we are all fighter types deep down, especially when it counts.

Epilogue

There are some who will say we'll never see anything like the good old days again. I don't necessarily agree, because the good old days for the young jet jockeys of today are happening right now. But I must admit, those early years for me and the renegades I ran into during the 50's and early 60's were awfully good.

Flying was a joy, something that I couldn't believe they paid me to do. Climbing into a single seated jet fighter plane is like reclining in your most comfortable chair. Every nook and cranny is familiar. When the safety harnesses are cinched down, you become a part of the overall system. All the switches and gages are within reach of the fingertips. It takes only a few smooth motions and the engine is at idle power. A quick jerk of your thumbs outward and the crew chief pulls out the chocks. A slight foward push on the throttle and the powerful machine is on it's way for take-off. Into position on the runway, throttle jammed forward to full power with brakes holding the quivering beast, then release. Such a surge of power, the head moves back as momentum increases, the backbone is becoming a part of the seat back, the sensation of speed is a reality. Getting airborne brings the ecstasy of knowing what real power can do to aluminum and steel. The earth rapidly falls away, and the feeling of freedom becomes overwhelming. Flicking the controls extends the brain impulses to unbounded extremes. Slight pressure to the right and the plane is in a right turn. Back on the stick and it seems the birds can't follow. Set the switches for weapons delivery, point the nose at the ground, pipper on the target, press the release button, and soar away. Target destroyed! That is why the machine was designed, the purpose has been fulfilled, head for home. The power still pulses, the controls still sensitive to a feather's touch. And, when the wheels again touch runway pavement, an overwhelming satisfaction seeps through the entire body. Back to earth for now, but the next time is already a vision in the reaches of the mind. Unconscious for the moment, but once the experience has been imbedded, there is no replacement. It beats sliced bread and other sensuous things all to pieces.

From the F-51 in flying school, the F-86 in Korea and Nellis, and the F-100 at Nellis and the Philippines, things seemed to be taken for granted without over reaction by the head guys. It seemed senses of humor were bigger, mistakes weren't that devastating, and there was better than strict regimentation to wake up to everyday. Like:

The night in flying school when a student landed a bit long in his F-51 and ran over the end of the runway onto the eighth green of the Craig AFB golf course. He gunned the powerful Rolls-Royce engine and blasted up an access road and back onto the ramp. No one noticed the mud and turf on the landing gear until the next morning. The greens keeper thought he had developed a bad case of gophers, the crew chief thought someone had used his aircraft as a plow, but there was no vast uproar or condemnation. The pilot did spend all his spare time before graduation as an assistant greens keeper (cutting grass) and as an assistant crew chief (washing airplanes). Who said an eye for an eye? Not anyone we knew! Or:

The brand new jet pilot in combat crew training enroute to Korea that got lost on a short night cross country and landed his F-86 in Mexico. Seems he was really turned around and went left instead of right at El Toro. With his fuel down to minimums, he spied a lighted runway in the dark unknown below. After a successful touch down, he was very surprised when it turned out to be a short dirt strip lighted by smudge pots. Back at Nellis, the squadron commander was fit to be tied when he learned that one of his charges had made such a stupid error. He immediately wanted to know if he had his wallet with him? Upon learning it was still in his locker, he said, "Leave him there overnight, we'll get him in the morning". With no money, the lost aviator's hotel for the night was the intake of his F-86. His thirfty (and uncomfortable) night was his retribution. You couldn't get out of going to Korea that easy. Or:

The Kimpo pilot who ran out of fuel upon returning from an extended combat sortie. On downwind, just prior to turning base, the "E" on the F-86 fuel gage wasn't kidding. The runway was almost within reach, but alas, the plane hit several thousand feet short. When the dust settled, our intrepid pilot stepped out of the cockpit with nary a scratch. Of course, there hadn't been any fire or explosion, although the aircraft wouldn't be flyable anytime soon. Without fuel, it's hard to have a good size bonfire. The stunned aviator was greeted with open arms and scheduled for the next day's mission. You didn't get court martialed or time off for being a bit short of the normal parking slot. This was war, not some 'mickey mouse' exercise that gets over supervised. Sometimes the real picture is overlooked. Some leaders do what they think someone higher up wants them to do, not what they should do. Luckily there were some real leaders in the 4th Fighter Wing.

Under current conditions, there would have been two less pilots in the force. One before he even graduated and the other before he got his chance at combat. For the zero fuel incident, it would have cost the flight leader and maybe the squadron commander their jobs. A committee might still be meeting to help determine further culpability, let's not make a prompt decision.

The frustrated golfer came out of Korea with an Air Force Cross, the 'South of the Border' aviator was credited with three kills and two damages, and the glider pilot went on to get his star. Wouldn't it have been a shame not to have had that second chance?

If a person is loyal, conscientious, and dedicated, they deserve more than one time at bat. That second chance could really produce a winner.

Keep that 'Fighter Pilot Spirit' alive, do good work, and enjoy life; it's the one thing that only comes along once!